D1006755

PUBLIC
FAITH IN
ACTION

PUBLIC FAITH IN ACTION

How to Think Carefully, Engage Wisely, and Vote with Integrity

MIROSLAV VOLF AND RYAN McANNALLY-LINZ

BrazosPress
a division of Baker Publishing Group
Grand Rapids, Michigan

© 2016 by Miroslav Volf and Ryan McAnnally-Linz

Published by Brazos Press
a division of Baker Publishing Group
P.O. Box 6287, Grand Rapids, MI 49516-6287
www.brazospress.com

Published in association with The Martell Agency

Printed in the United States of America

Library of Congress Cataloging-in-Publication Data is on file at the Library of Congress, Washington, DC.

ISBN 978-1-58743-384-9

16 17 18 19 20 21 22   7 6 5 4 3 2 1

To Jürgen Moltmann,
for your ninetieth birthday

CONTENTS

INTRODUCTION

This book grew out of a series of Facebook posts designed to help guide Christians in the United States through the maze of issues that were debated during the presidential election in 2012. The posts found global resonance (they were even published independently in an Italian translation), and they did so partly because they, like the present book, addressed the US situation but weren't tied too closely to it. Instead, they offered a Christian perspective on issues of interest in many parts of the world. The posts appeared on Miroslav Volf's Facebook page, but Ryan McAnnally-Linz was closely involved in their drafting. When Brazos Press expressed interest in publishing them in revised and expanded form, we decided to coauthor the book.

As its title suggests, this work is a companion volume to *A Public Faith: How Followers of Christ Should Serve the Common Good* (2011). The goal of *A Public Faith*, which sums up in accessible form results from many years of Miroslav's research and for which Ryan served as research assistant, was to explore the place and the role of followers of Christ in pluralistic societies today. It argued against both exclusion of religions from public space and saturation of public space by a single religion. It sketched a vision of a publicly engaged Christian faith that affirms pluralism as a political project, and it argued that the Christian faith's deepest convictions support just such an approach to public engagement.[1] The present volume continues where the first ends. It explores what kind of virtues and commitments should inform the public engagement of the followers of Christ. Hence the title: *Public Faith in Action*. For responsible public action we need what these two books together provide: a vision of the place and the role of Christians in today's pluralistic societies and an articulation of the relevant virtues and commitments that should guide them.

Before you read the book, it's important for us to clarify what we mean by "public." As we see it, the word *public* doesn't name an isolated part of human life that can be dropped into its own little basket next to other baskets for family life, church life, club life, and so on. The public can't be neatly separated out and dealt with apart from the rest of life, as we might separate the whites from the colors when we do laundry. That said, the public doesn't swallow up the rest of life either. It's not just another word for the whole of life. Rather, the public is one dimension or aspect of human life, the one that involves issues and institutions concerning the good of all, the common good. The public is life seen as life *together* in society. Correspondingly, public faith is faith concerned with responsible shaping of our common life and common world.[2]

Every part of life has a public side. All of life is shot through with public significance. Sometimes this public side is obvious, as when a person votes or runs for office. Other times, it's harder to discern but is there nonetheless, as when someone decides whether to send her children to private rather than public school. Even the shape of our most intimate desires says something about and makes a difference for our common life.

Public life isn't just for politicians or celebrities. Each and every one of us lives a public life because every life has a public dimension running through it. Every life contributes, however faintly, to public life writ large: governments, economies, educational institutions, media, and the like. So it's not just that anyone and everyone *can* engage in public life; we all inescapably do so. To take an extreme example, when devoted Christians left their homes and families and possessions to dwell as solitary monks in the deserts of third-century Egypt, they saw themselves as withdrawing from the "world." But even that withdrawal was a public act. It communicated just how far, in their opinion, the society of the time fell short of the demands of the gospel. If today you decided to give up on "politics"—to stop voting, to quit reading the headlines, to studiously avoid conversations about taxes and health care, to hunker down and just go about your business as best you could—you wouldn't be entirely escaping from public life. Rather, you would be living a certain kind of public life, a limited, largely passive, and likely irresponsible public life, but a public life nonetheless.

This book is primarily about *active* public life, not about the passive public life we might lead by saying nothing and doing nothing about things of common concern. This book is about the public lives of ordinary disciples of Jesus Christ and the public goods those lives should promote. It's about the Christ-centered convictions that should shape our judgments and also the Christlike character that should shine in our actions. It's about faithfulness at the ballot box and at the neighborhood association meeting. It's about the big issues of national and international affairs—migration, tax policies, war and peace—and about the small contributions to a flourishing public life we make with our attitudes, our purchases, and our conversations.

The book is divided into three parts. Part 1 discusses the big-picture *commitments* that orient faithful Christian public life. Reading this part first will help you put later chapters in context, but we've written the book so that you can dip into chapters one by one if there are some questions that interest you more than others.

Part 2 examines the *convictions* that should shape our engagement with specific matters of public significance. Some of these chapters contain fairly definite recommendations about public policy, but their overall purpose is not to lay out a policy platform; rather, it is to sketch out how life together and its institutional implementations might look today if they reflected, however brokenly, the coming kingdom of God. Each chapter in part 2 starts with a succinct formulation of a relevant conviction, something we can keep in mind as we advocate for a policy or assess a candidate for a public office. The main body of the chapter seeks to explain and justify the conviction. The chapter ends with a section called "Room for Debate" that presents questions that remain open even if you're convinced by the rest of the chapter. These questions show that there are usually several steps between the convictions we're discussing and the sort of proposals you're likely to hear on the campaign trail.

Part 3 considers some of the virtues, or qualities of *character*, that we ought to develop and live out in our public lives. Faithfulness to Christ is about more than having the right beliefs and doing the right things. It's about being formed into a certain pattern of character so that we become witnesses to Christ in the whole of our lives.

This book could have been a lot longer than it is. It covers quite a bit of ground in a few pages. We have intentionally kept it short—with each chapter offering a quick guide through some of the most important issues facing the world today. There is, of course, much more that can be (and has been) said about everything we've written on. We've done our best to give you a solid foundation for thinking through these issues, but reading this book won't make you an expert on any of them. To help get you started if you want to dig deeper into any of the subjects we discuss, we've provided a short guide at the end of each chapter, an annotated list of a few articles and books on the chapter's subject (most of which were prepared by a pair of extraordinary researchers, Ryan Darr and Toni Alimi). We hope you'll pick up a couple of the resources on these lists as you continue to explore what it means to put your public faith into action.

We've written this book from within particular contexts. For instance, we both reside in the Northeast of the United States, we both have lived in non-Western countries, and we both come from and belong to streams within the Protestant movement in Christianity. These contexts have inevitably shaped what we write. That's as it must be. To speak as a human being is to speak from a particular place at a particular time. To author a wide-ranging book such as *Public Faith in Action* is also to write as a nonexpert. That, too, is as it must be. We live in an exceedingly complex world, and knowledge about it is highly specialized. Public engagement as citizens of modern democracies, however, requires us to know what bearing Christian faith has on all aspects of life. We are all amateurs when it comes to at least some aspects of public life.

Writing a book constrained by limits of both location and expertise is a risky, open-ended venture, one that invites readers to join the endeavor—to interpret the text from their angles and for their places, to supplement, to amend, and even to contradict. More generally, understanding any text or any speech is not a matter of seeing a fixed, unchanging essence that the words express but rather a question of "knowing how to 'go on,'" as Rowan Williams puts it, echoing the philosopher Ludwig Wittgenstein (1889–1951). To understand is to be able to interact, to carry a conversation forward.[3] In writing this book, our goal is not to end a conversation but to enrich it, not to achieve passive submission but to invite critical discussion.

We hope that our reflections will be relevant and helpful for people trying to serve Christ in many different places and situations. It is, however, up to *you*, the reader, to discern how our arguments and stances relate to your communities as well as to discern things to which limitations of context and expertise, and even our sinfulness, have blinded us. Take this book as an invitation to conversation. If you're not convinced by something we say, try to convince us (and others). If you are convinced, tell us (and others) what it means for you and your communities. Above all, take the book as an invitation to action: see what happens when you follow Christ into public engagement.

PART 1

COMMITMENTS

1

CHRIST THE CENTER
AND NORM

A basic commitment underlies this book: Christian faith has an inalienable public dimension. Christians aren't Christ's followers just in their private and communal lives; they are Christ's followers in their public and political lives as well. Christ must be the center and norm for Christian public engagement because Christ and his Spirit are at work, not just in our hearts, families, and churches, but also in our nations and the entire world. We don't need to waste words defending this commitment; most Christians today embrace it. But it is important to be clear about what the commitment means, for it both sets the course of Christian public engagement and places limits on it.

At first glance Jesus Christ seems a remarkably odd choice for the role of determining the shape of our political lives. He calls "blessed" those who are meek, the pure of heart, and the persecuted (Matt. 5:5, 8, 10). He stoops down to wash his disciples' feet (John 13:1–17), he often shies away from public attention (e.g., Matt. 8:4; Mark 1:43–45), and he rebukes his followers for trying to use the sword (the classic symbol of political power) to rescue him from an unjust arrest (Matt. 26:52; Luke 22:51; John 18:11). His whole way of speaking, his bearing, and his mannerisms often seem unworldly, more saintly than kingly. And his message seems, frankly, too radical to apply to political life. "Turn to them the other cheek," he says (Matt. 5:39 NIV). "Do not judge" (Matt. 7:1). "Love your enemies" (Matt. 5:44). How could any of that possibly have something relevant to say to the rough-and-tumble, publicity-seeking, deal-making world of public life and engagement?

On closer examination, however, Jesus's life and message are unmistakably public, even political, though not in the usual sense of the term. After all, the core of Jesus's preaching is that "the kingdom of God has come near" (Matt. 4:17; Mark 1:15). What-ever else it might be, *kingdom* is surely a political term. In line with the political character of the kingdom, the book of Reve-lation portrays the final advent of God's reign as the "holy city, the new Jerusalem, coming down out of heaven from God" to be established on earth (Rev. 21:2). We get our word *political* from the Greek word for "city" in that verse (*polis*).

Christ, the Spirit, and the Kingdom

On its own, Jesus's delivering the message of the kingdom wouldn't justify our making *Jesus himself* the norm for public engagement. Couldn't Jesus have been just a prophet of the kingdom, merely sketching a vision of it, or a philosopher of the kingdom, merely explaining and justifying its constitution? Or might he be an ex-ample for us to follow? In fact, he is more than that. The king-dom Christ proclaimed is inseparable from who he was during his ministry and crucifixion and who he continues to be after his resurrection. Jesus insisted on a close tie between himself and the kingdom. Rejecting the charge that he cast out demons by Satan's power, he said, "If it is by the finger of God that I cast out the demons, then the kingdom of God has come to you" (Luke 11:20).

The kingdom has come in Jesus's own activity. You cannot have the kingdom without having Jesus Christ; you cannot have Jesus Christ without having the kingdom. Consequently, his entire life is of public import.

As Jürgen Moltmann has argued in *The Crucified God*, Jesus's "way to the cross" was a path of conflict with the religious and political rulers of his day, who saw his teaching, his ministry, and his very life as a threat.[1] From Herod's desperate attempt to kill the infant Christ to the Romans crucifying him for insurrection under the mocking sign, "This is Jesus, the King of the Jews" (Matt. 27:37), the powers that be considered him a problem to be dealt with, violently if need be. Expanding on Moltmann's thesis, Michael Welker has shown that Christ was crucified under the auspices of a broader set of public institutions and agents—not just religion and politics but also law and public opinion.[2] Their role in the crucifixion reveals just how susceptible to corruption these structures of human life are. Christ's entering the conflict with them, making the conflict part of his mission, and engaging in it in his own way marked by nonviolence brings the corruption of the public structures of human life under God's judgment.

The way the conflict between Christ and public institutions and agents of his day turned out might seem to leave little room for Christ to serve as the norm for political engagements. After all, he seemed to have been defeated. But in fact, the conflict serves as a model for his followers in their own times and places. For Christ's death on the cross was a *central victory* in a series of victories over corrupted forms of human life. In the Acts of the Apostles, we read that "God raised him up" and that he now sits "at the right hand of God" and pours out the Spirit so that his mission can continue in the world (Acts 2:24, 33).

Christ, then, is alive and at work in the world through the Spirit. His death did not expose him as a false pretender to kingly rule, nor did it bring his rule to an end. To the contrary, Jesus's resurrection and ascension confirm and establish his rule in a new way. Christ is exalted into universal lordship, a lordship that is "far above all rule and authority and power and dominion" (Eph. 1:21). In the image of 1 Corinthians 15, he governs the kingdom until its eschatological fulfillment, when he will hand it over to the Father. As the conflict-heavy language of this passage ("after he has destroyed every ruler and every authority and power" [v. 24]) and Colossians 2:15 suggests, Christ's mission remains one of resistance to sin, unmasking the corruptions and pretensions of earthly powers. But it is also one of bringing about foretastes of the kingdom in history. Christ works not only against but also within institutions and agents concerned with common life. Sin corrupts them, but Christ is at work redeeming them.

The kingdom that Jesus brought near is radically different from run-of-the-mill political regimes. It wasn't established as one more kingdom alongside others in the way that Rome was founded in 753 BC and then struggled for supremacy with Carthage and other political powers. Nor did it succeed other regimes in the way that one government administration follows another. Rather, the kingdom is the ultimate goal of all history and all creation. It is the fulfillment to which everything is being drawn. It is the indescribable future when God will be all in all (1 Cor. 15:28).[3] This kingdom is not only final (it can never be undone) and universal (it will extend across the whole creation), but it is also all-encompassing. It *includes* but also far *exceeds* all that we usually classify as "public," its reach extending from our most intimate desires to the fate of the entire cosmos.

Christ and Public Engagement

All this is not to say, however, that there is no difference between Christ's work in the church and in the wider world. Karl Barth (1886–1968) provides a helpful image for understanding what the universal work of Christ means for the relationship between Christians, the church, and political societies. Christ, he says, is like the center of two concentric circles. The smaller circle is the Christian community, which knows that Christ is the center and aims to live in light of that knowledge. The larger circle is the civil community, which has Christ as its center even though it may not know it. Christ's rule in the outer circle is neither identical with nor completely different from his rule in the inner circle, but it is analogous to it.[4] As a *community*, the church is of major public significance, a point many theologians have made in recent decades. But the edges of the church are not the limits of Christian public engagement. As participants in the civil community, Christians strive to bring it into greater conformity to the character and rule of Christ.

Christians ought to be active in the "outer circle" because *Christ calls us to follow him in our whole lives and to work in the power of the Spirit wherever he is at work.* Throughout the Gospel stories of his life, Jesus calls people to follow him, to orient their lives around him, in ways that leave no part of their lives untouched. Discipleship affects family life (Matt. 10:37). It affects relationships with wealth and possessions (Matt. 6:24; Luke 16:13). It affects work (Mark 1:16–17). It affects social life (Matt. 5:42–48). And so on. The point is: if we are committed to following Jesus in the power of the Spirit, we are committed to letting him determine the character of our whole lives—no exceptions. We are his disciples in our judgments, words, and deeds that affect the common good, just as we are his disciples in every other aspect of our lives.

Commitment to public engagement as Christ's disciples draws us to the Scriptures as the touchstone for discerning Christ at work. Christ in the world cannot be different from Christ in the Scriptures. For *Christ always remains true to himself*: "Jesus Christ is the same yesterday and today and forever" (Heb. 13:8). His character as we see it in Scripture is consistent with his character always and everywhere. Granted, we should expect Christ to surprise us—not just because we can never fully comprehend him but also because the situations in which he is at work are changing. To give the same talk to two different audiences is to give two different talks; to act in the same way in two different situations is to act in two different ways. Nevertheless, we can be confident that Christ will never turn on a dime and become someone antithetical to the Christ we see in Scripture. For example, in market economies he won't command acquisitiveness instead of generosity; in bureaucratized social-service systems he won't say that compassion is obsolete; and to citizens under threat from terrorists he won't claim that it's just fine to hate those enemies instead of loving them.

Putting all these observations together results in the following line of thought: Because (a) Christ is working everywhere bringing about anticipations of the kingdom of God, (b) we are called to follow wherever Christ is working, and (c) the character of Christ as testified to in Scripture faithfully expresses his character as it is always and everywhere, we can conclude that (d) *the person of Jesus as we encounter him in Scripture and discern him at work today through the Spirit is the norm for our public engagement.*

Although Jesus brought the kingdom of God in his life, death, and resurrection, the kingdom will be fully actualized only at the end of history. We live, therefore, within a field of tension: the kingdom is in some sense actual "now," but in another sense it is still "not yet." The transition to the full actuality of the kingdom of God is not a matter of gradual progress within history as we know it. Rather, the change is so stark that Scripture talks about it as a "new creation" that God makes out of the "old" one (2 Cor. 5:17; Isa. 65:17). Consequently, we shouldn't think of any human community, whether the church or a civic community, as progressively "expanding" the kingdom of God on earth, as some conquering force might. For the most part, Christians have rightly abandoned the false dream, associated with progressivist accounts of history, that if we just keep working at it, eventually, one stone at a time, we will build the New Jerusalem. According to the book of Revelation, the holy city must *come down from God* (Rev. 21:2).

Our primary stance toward the kingdom, therefore, ought to be one of hope, an eager expectation that God will bring to completion the kingdom work begun in Christ's incarnation and continued through the Spirit. To hope isn't merely to dream, of course. To hope is to live into the reality of the kingdom that we hope for. That kingdom is the fundamental aim of human existence and the deepest longing of human hearts. Those who follow Christ in the power of the Spirit should let it determine the character of their lives and their projects. Even though we cannot make the kingdom arrive, our lives and our world, including our political societies and global realities, can reflect some of its character. In the next chapter, we will briefly explore that character and how we can reflect it.

Resources for Further Reflection

Introductory Reading

Evans, Rachel Held. "Are the Teachings of Jesus Too Radical for Public Policy?" *Rachel Held Evans* (blog), April 22, 2009. http://rachelheldevans.com/blog/jesusandtorture?rq=public. Prompted by discussions with friends about poverty and torture, Evans critiques the tendency to let other scriptural passages trump Jesus's teachings in Christian debates about public issues but also wonders whether Jesus's teachings might actually be too radical for earthly public life.

Stringfellow, William. *A Private and Public Faith*. Eugene, OR: Wipf & Stock, 1999. Stringfellow makes a compelling argument that the task of Christian life is to discern and follow the Word of God (Christ) in the common life of the world.

Volf, Miroslav. *A Public Faith: How Followers of Christ Should Serve the Common Good*. Grand Rapids: Brazos, 2011. This book collects and synthesizes Miroslav's reflections on the stance that followers of Christ should take toward public life, arguing in particular against idleness and coerciveness and for thoughtful engagement.

Advanced Study

Barth, Karl. "The Christian Community and the Civil Community." In *Community, Church, and State: Three Essays*, 149–89. Eugene, OR: Wipf & Stock, 2004. One of the most influential theologians of the twentieth century offers an account of the relationship between the church and civil communities and a vision for responsible, faithful Christian public engagement.

Mathewes, Charles. *A Theology of Public Life.* Cambridge: Cambridge University Press, 2007. Building in particular on the thought of St. Augustine, Mathewes argues that public engagement enriches Christian faith.

Moltmann, Jürgen. *Theology of Hope.* Minneapolis: Fortress, 1993. Moltmann's groundbreaking book reoriented theological reflection toward the expectation of the coming kingdom of God. It concludes with reflections on the public implications of Christian hope.

Tanner, Kathryn. "Politics." In *Christ the Key*, 207–46. Cambridge: Cambridge University Press, 2010. In line with the title of her book, Tanner argues that Christ's ways of relating to the Father and the Spirit, as well as to other humans, are key for understanding what Christian engagement with political communities should look like.

2

CHRIST, THE SPIRIT, AND FLOURISHING

The Christian faith is a public faith. The reason is simple: the work of Christ has an inalienable public dimension; it did so two thousand years ago, when Christ walked on the streets of Palestine and hung on the cross outside the walls of Jerusalem, and it does so now, when he sits on the heavenly throne above all powers. That's not to say that the Christian faith is a "political religion," a religion celebrating the unity of moral order and political rule in a society, furnishing political rule and its juridical order with a theological justification. Christ, the universal king of the kingdom that is for this world but not from it, is the end of such political religion. That same Christ is also the beginning of a publicly engaged faith.[1]

Following Christ in the Spirit

What is the relation between Christ the universal king and his publicly engaged followers? In chapter 1 we argued that Christ is our norm. As norm, Christ might be seen as "behind us" in first-century Palestine or "above us" at the right hand of the Father, issuing commands to obey and offering an ideal to live up to. Both these ways of thinking about how Christ relates to us—the commander and the model—are true but inadequate. The relationship between Christ and his followers is much more intimate. In his short but highly influential text *The Freedom of a Christian*, Martin Luther (1483–1546) suggested boldly that Christians are "Christs" to their neighbors.[2] We don't just obey and imitate Christ, who is outside us; we embody Christ, who is present *in* us.

One way to think of embodying Christ is to see the church, the visible body of Christ, as the continuing incarnation of Christ. But that is to relate Christ and Christians *too* intimately, in fact so much so that the church threatens to squeeze out and replace Christ. A sounder way to think about embodying Christ is to see the church and individual Christians as *continuing Christ's anointing with the Holy Spirit.*[3] The same Spirit who descended on Christ (Matt. 3:16–17; John 1:32–33), anointing him to bring good news to the poor (Luke 4:18), is sent by the resurrected Christ to rest on Christ's followers (John 20:22; Acts 1:5; 2:1–4). Called as Christ's followers, we are, like Christ, sent in the power of Christ's Spirit. Through the Spirit, Christ is with us and in us, and we are in Christ (Matt. 28:20; John 15:4; Rom. 8:1, 10–11; 2 Cor. 1:21–22).[4]

In the previous chapter we stressed that the rule of Christ is not limited to the church, the community of Christ's followers. The same is true of the work of the Spirit. The outpouring of the Spirit at Pentecost inaugurated and anticipated God's final gift of the Spirit to "all flesh" (Acts 2:17; Joel 2:28), even if we don't yet see the fruit of the Spirit everywhere manifest. Similarly, in the life of a Christian, the work of the Spirit is as comprehensive as the rule of Christ, encompassing every part and dimension of life. The Spirit is at work in the entire world; and the entire life of the Christian, in all its dimensions, is life in the Spirit.[5]

What does the Spirit seek in energizing and guiding Christians, in making them "Christs" to their neighbors with their individual as well as the common good in view? What was the Spirit seeking in descending on Christ? The goal of Christ's Spirit-anointed mission to establish the kingdom was for human beings and the entire creation to *flourish*. Life in the everlasting kingdom of God is what all of us were made for. The kingdom is the perfection of the "abundant life" that Christ came to bring (John 10:10).

The Three Aspects of Flourishing

Since we take "flourishing" to be what Christ's rule and the Spirit's presence are about, we've made it the central organizing idea of this book. We use the term somewhat loosely as a very rough equivalent to "the good life" or "the life worth living." It is important to spell out what we mean by "flourishing" and how it is rooted in and displayed in the life and teachings of Christ. We will do so in greater detail in the course of the book, but here at the beginning it is crucial to identify and explain the three formal aspects of flourishing. They are (1) leading life well, (2) life going well, and (3) life feeling good.[6] The first two especially, on their own and in relation to one another, will play a critical role in the remainder of the book. The three correspond roughly to three important strands of thinking about the good life in the Western tradition, each strand emphasizing in its own way one facet but never fully disregarding the other two. Immanuel Kant's (1724–1804) ethics of duty places stress on leading life well; Karl Marx's (1818–83) revolutionary vision highlights life going well; much of contemporary popular culture stresses happiness as life feeling good.

Leading life well concerns how you conduct yourself in the world. It's a matter of receiving God's gifts well, having the right dispositions, judging well, and acting rightly, regardless of the circumstances. Christ sums up the well-led life under the heading of *love*: "'You shall love the Lord your God with all your heart, and with all your soul, and with all your mind.' This is the greatest and first commandment. And a second is like it: 'You shall love your neighbor as yourself.' On these two commandments hang all the law and the prophets" (Matt. 22:37–40; cf. Rom. 12:9–10; Gal. 5:14; James 2:8; 1 John 4:21). Christ not only preached love but also lived it out perfectly. He loved the Father (John 14:31) and loved humanity with the greatest love there is (John 15:12–13; cf. Gal. 2:20).

Life going well means, roughly, that the circumstances of one's life are genuinely good. Whereas leading life well is a matter of our own agency,[7] life going well depends in great part on circumstances beyond our control—what neighborhood we're raised in, whether we're genetically predisposed to serious diseases, whether our homeland is at peace or torn apart by war, whether we live in cultures with high or low levels of trust, and so on. In word and deed Jesus demonstrates that it's important for life to go well. He heals the sick and delivers the spiritually oppressed (Mark 1:29–34). He feeds the hungry (Matt. 14:13–21). He restores sons to their widowed mothers, and brothers to their sisters (Luke 7:11–15; John 11:1–44). Jesus doesn't treat humans as one-dimensional creatures who can fully flourish no matter what the circumstances so long as they are virtuous. He says, "Strive first for the kingdom of God and his righteousness," but then he goes on to say, "and all these things"—food, clothing, shelter, security, and the like—"will be given to you as well" because "your heavenly Father knows that you need all these things" (Matt. 6:32–33). We can sum up what it means for life to go well with the idea of *peace*, understood in the sense of the Hebrew *shalom*, which encompasses "good health, a sense of well-being, good fortune, the cohesiveness of the community, relationship to relatives and their state of being, and anything else deemed necessary for everything to be in order."[8] Obviously, in important ways life did not go well for Jesus himself: he did not have a "place to lay his head" (Matt. 8:20 NIV), he was persecuted, and eventually he was brutally killed (perhaps the right word is *murdered*, because Pilate never pronounced judgment against Jesus but merely "handed him over to be crucified" [Matt. 27:26]).[9] And yet that is not the end of the story, for the risen Christ was restored to the glory he shared with God from the foundation of the world.

Life feeling good refers to the affective dimension of human flourishing. For a human being to truly flourish, it is not enough to live well a life that goes well. Imagine someone standing at the altar about to marry a perfect match, she and the groom both in excellent health with a robust community of friends and family to support them, each of them having treated the other with respect and tenderness—and the bride feeling no happiness. Something would be missing. It would seem somehow off to say she was flourishing. A proper emotional response to ourselves, to the world as we find it, and to God is vital to our flourishing. The paradigmatic emotion of flourishing life is *joy*. In true joy, we receive the world (or part of it) as a blessing and respond accordingly. Such joy marks the whole arc of Christ's life and mission. Christ's birth is "good news of great joy for all the people" (Luke 2:10), and his resurrection inspires joy in his disciples (Matt. 28:8). Joy is the last experience the disciples have in the presence of Christ and at the same time the first state of the newborn church: the disciples worshiped the ascended Jesus "and returned to Jerusalem with great joy" (Luke 24:52). Joy, we can say, sums up what life in the kingdom feels like.

In a significant way true joy gathers all three facets of flourishing and stands for the kingdom itself, as when in Jesus's parable of the talents the master says to the good and trustworthy servants, "Enter into the joy of your master" (Matt. 25:21–23). In their own way, of course, true peace (Isa. 11:1–11) and authentic love (1 Cor. 13:13) gather all three facets of flourishing as well. Though distinct, the three facets are intimately related to one another. Each influences the others in ways that can create either virtuous or vicious circles among them. When things are going well, loving others can feel like running downhill. And we all know that life can go rather badly even though we lead it well; indeed, life can go terribly badly just *because* we are leading it well, as the case of Jesus's crucifixion illustrates. Yet, despite the disorder of a sinful world, there are plenty of times when doing the right thing winds up shaping our circumstances for the better. Conversely, if you abscond with your company's money, use it to buy a new sports car, and take a 120 mph joyride down the highway, soon enough your life will stop going well. Chances are, it won't feel very good either. The influence can go the other way too. It's painfully common to observe the circumstances of our lives eating away at our spiritual strength, threatening to undercut our ability to live life well, and draining joy out of our lives.

In such cycles, the most important element is leading life well. While it is not entirely independent of the other two, it is the point in the cycle where we have the most say. That's true even in the bleakest of circumstances and darkest of emotions—though, of course, we all need to be liberated from the captivities of our will, and there are cases in which we are utterly powerless, the starkest one in the New Testament being demon possession. In Christ's life we see how a friend's betrayal, his impending arrest, and the anguish of a looming execution threaten to overwhelm him. And yet Christ's prayer in Gethsemane not only reaffirms the goodness of life going well ("If it is possible, let this cup pass from me") but also enacts a commitment to live well, in faithful love, come what may ("Yet not what I want but what you want" [Matt. 26:39]), as well as hope that joy will come, suffering and shame notwithstanding (Heb. 12:2).

Christ does not merely lead life well as an example for others but actually draws human beings into the goodness of his life and empowers them to flourish. And that brings us back to the work of the Spirit, where we began this chapter. The Spirit whom Christ sends—the very Spirit who rested on Christ and empowered him to proclaim, enact, and embody the kingdom—yields fruit across all the facets of human flourishing: "The fruit of the Spirit is love, joy, peace . . ." (Gal. 5:22). The kingdom of God is "righteousness and peace and joy in the Holy Spirit," says Paul (Rom. 14:17). This is the kind of life we are called to. This is the kind of life—for our neighbors as much as for ourselves—toward which our engagements with all aspects of public life should aim.

Before we take up the convictions and virtues needed for responsible public engagement, we need to explore in the next chapter how to deal with the major differences—a gulf, some would say—that separate Jesus's time and ours. Even though Jesus is our norm, we cannot mechanically imitate Jesus, do simply and exactly what Jesus did. Here, too, the Spirit is the key. The Spirit makes Christ's followers to be "Christs" to others; the Spirit can therefore guide us as we discern how to be "Christs" in a world that, powered by rapid technological advances, is swiftly spinning away from resemblance to the world of first-century Palestine.

Resources for Further Reflection

Introductory Reading

Crouch, Andy. "What's So Great about 'The Common Good'?" *Christianity Today*, October 12, 2012. http://www.christianity today.com/ct/2012/november/whats-so-great-about-common -good.html. Crouch explores the history of the idea of the common good and its link to human flourishing. He argues that it's a crucial category for Christian public engagement today.

Volf, Miroslav. "The Crown of the Good Life: Joy, Happiness, and the Good Life, A Hypothesis." *Big Questions Online*, October 21, 2014. https://www.bigquestionsonline.com/content/what -difference-between-joy-and-happiness. Miroslav analyzes the idea of joy and argues that it is the "crown of the good life" because true joy integrates leading life well, life going well, and life feeling right.

Wright, N. T., and Miroslav Volf. "The Political Significance of Joy." Yale Center for Faith and Culture video, 19:48. Posted September 29, 2014. http://faith.yale.edu/news/political-signi ficance-joy-nt-wright-theology-joy. Wright discusses how the resurrection of Jesus Christ shapes a Christian understanding of joy and claims that this joy contrasts with common under-standings of power and politics.

Advanced Study

Volf, Miroslav, and Justin E. Crisp, eds. *Joy and Human Flourish-ing: Essays on Theology, Culture, and the Good Life*. Minneapo-lis: Fortress, 2015. This collection of essays by thinkers such as Jürgen Moltmann and N. T. Wright examines the place of joy in flourishing human life. Together the essays offer biblical, theo-logical, ethical, social, economic, and pastoral perspectives on joy and demonstrate the centrality of joy to the Christian faith.

Volf, Miroslav, and Maurice Lee. "The Spirit and the Church." In *Advents of the Spirit: An Introduction to the Current Study of Pneumatology*, edited by Bradford E. Hinze and D. Lyle Dabney, 380–407. Milwaukee: Marquette University Press, 2001. This essay is an extended exploration of the idea that the church is the continuation not of Christ's incarnation but of his anoint-ing with the Spirit.

Yale Center for Faith and Culture. "Christ and Human Flourishing (2014)." http://faith.yale.edu/god-human-flourishing/christ-and -human-flourishing-2014. In this collection of papers, theo-logians and biblical scholars explore the connection between human flourishing and Christ's person and work.

3

READING IN CONTEXTS

Jesus Christ is the norm of Christian public engagement. But what does that mean concretely, when we face a particular issue, whether it is inequality of wealth, the legality of abortion, or the nature of religious freedom? The process of discerning how we should engage as followers of Christ in the public square is a bit like reading or interpreting a text. To read well in general, we need to pay attention to context—to the place of a word or a sentence in a larger work and to that work's own larger setting. When it comes to Christ and Christian engagement for the common good, there are two contexts we need to keep in mind. The first is the context of the Gospel narratives within Scripture. We'll call this "canonical context," since the traditional name for the collection of books that make up the Bible is the "canon." The second is the context of our own lives, the particularities of the current situation. We'll call this "contemporary context."

Canonical Context

Paying attention to canonical context means going back and forth between reading every part of Scripture in light of the New

Testament testimonies about Jesus Christ and reading the New Testament witness to Jesus Christ in light of the entire Bible. Take, first, reading all of Scripture in light of Jesus Christ. Since the birth, life, death, and resurrection of Jesus Christ are both the definitive revelation of God and the decisive event in God's redeeming work in the world, the New Testament texts that witness to them are the heart of the canon. They ought to exert a kind of gravitational pull on Christian reading of other parts of Scripture. In the Sermon on the Mount, Jesus says, "You have heard that it was said to those of ancient times . . . But I say to you . . ." (Matt. 5:21–22). This authoritative "But I say to you" means that Jesus is the new Moses and that his word is above the authority of the Hebrew Bible. When faced with apparent conflicts between some part of Scripture and the New Testament witnesses to Jesus Christ, the latter take priority. For instance, American settlers interpreted the command that the Israelites "must utterly destroy" the Canaanites when they entered the promised land to require (or at least permit) them to exterminate those who stood in the way of what they deemed to be God's plans for their colonies (see Deut. 7:2). But giving priority to the New Testament witnesses to Jesus's life rules out any such interpretation. Loving your enemies and exterminating them do *not* go together. For Christians there is no scriptural warrant for massacring those who stand between us and our personal or collective "promised land."[1]

At the same time, we also need to reverse the process and situate the New Testament witness to Jesus Christ in the context of the Bible as a whole. After all, Jesus himself said that he came not to abrogate the law and God's promises but to fulfill them. You cannot understand what fulfillment is unless you connect it to what is being fulfilled. Correspondingly, the Hebrew Bible continued to be *the* Bible of the early church and became part of the authoritative canon for the church throughout the ages. If we forget this, we will misconstrue what it means for Jesus Christ to be the norm of judgments and engagements that concern the common good.

For example, when Jesus talks about what we would call "economic" matters, his concern often focuses on the plight of the poor. Luke's version of the Beatitudes includes "Blessed are you who are poor, for yours is the kingdom of God" (Luke 6:20) and comes with the symmetrical saying, "Woe to you who are rich, for you have received your consolation" (Luke 6:24). On their own, these and similar passages could easily lead us to think that *distribution* of goods is all that matters. A careful reading of the Gospels, however, shows that they presuppose the *production* of goods through human labor. Alongside the stress on just distribution, the production side of economics gets a much fuller and more explicit treatment in the Hebrew Scriptures, beginning right at, well, the beginning, when "the LORD God took the man and put him in the garden of Eden to till it and keep it" (Gen. 2:15). As we move back to the Gospels, and to the New Testament more broadly, with the concerns of the Hebrew Bible in mind, the background of production comes into sharper focus. Even in a story such as Jesus feeding the five thousand (Matt. 14:13–21), in which the accent falls heavily on God's marvelous provision, it is bread that came from human tilling of the land and fish caught through human labor that are multiplied.

Contemporary Context

The last book of the Bible was written sometime around the end of the first century. The world has changed dramatically in the meantime. To discern the public significance of Christ today, we have to identify ways that our own situations differ from the social world in which the Gospels are set and to which they originally spoke, and we have to discern what bearing those differences have for our judgments and actions. There is no easy, color-by-numbers protocol for moving between Scripture's world and ours. Doing so is a matter of practical wisdom. It is fraught with uncertainty and risk, and it ought to involve a great deal of trust in and attentiveness to the Spirit, who rested on Christ throughout his earthly life and ministry, through whom the church and individual Christians participate in Christ's mission in the world, and who mysteriously guides and energizes all that is true, good, and beautiful in the world.

We will encounter many differences of historical context in the course of the book, but here we need to highlight three general features of many contemporary contexts: the popularity of the democratic ideal, the emergence of complex social systems, and astounding technological development. These three features make our present situation markedly different from the contexts in which Jesus lived and the Bible was written.

1. *The democratic ideal.* Since the seventeenth century, the idea has gradually taken hold globally that "sovereignty," the legitimate source of political power, resides not with a monarch or an aristocratic class but with "the people." There are many different theories about how popular sovereignty works, but the general concept has become so widely accepted that even political regimes with only token democratic procedures feel compelled to appeal to the sovereignty of the people for their legitimacy. In probably the most incredible example, the official name of North Korea, the most autocratic regime on the planet, is the *Democratic People's Republic of Korea.*

The common acceptance of democratic sovereignty changes the widely shared answers to two important political questions: (1) To whom is obedience due? (2) Who are the proper agents of political and social change? In the past, an emperor or queen might command personal allegiance and obedience. Now each citizen is a member of the sovereign people bound together to a constitution. As a consequence, Christian obedience to political authorities is not merely regulated by a more fundamental obedience to God but is also compatible with efforts to alter political society's course. Political change is no longer simply a top-down affair but a responsibility of all adult members of the community.

2. *Complex social systems*. Modern societies function to a great extent through complex, relatively impersonal structures that we might call, echoing the sociologist Max Weber (1864–1920), bureaucratic systems. These systems are differentiated (though not totally independent) from one another. Each follows its own rules and has its own dynamics and goals. The market dances to the rhythms of profits, electability sets the beat for politics, and so on. These structures resist attempts to use "outside" values to steer them. Moreover, any one individual working within them has limited responsibility and capacity to effect change. The much-talked-about phenomenon of globalization adds a further level of complication. The various political societies in the world today are bound together by systems of economic, political, and ecological interdependence. Changes in any one society can only accomplish so much, and the placement of each society in the interlocking global network limits the extent of these changes. If one country taxes businesses more in order to finance education and health care, businesses can migrate to another country where taxes are lower and leave people jobless; if one country limits disparities in wealth, wealthy individuals can move to another; and so on.

Both bureaucratization and globalization put significant strictures on what we can expect to be able to change. There is massive inertia in these systems. Our capacities for even understanding how they work, much less for directing them as we wish, are limited. Faithful public engagement in the face of these features of contemporary contexts requires that we be wise to the limits they impose while retaining a robust hope in the power of God's surprising activity to bring about foretastes of the kingdom where we would least expect them.

3. *Technological development*. We live in an age of astounding expansion of knowledge and of human ability to manipulate physical reality. This raises a host of moral questions, many of them a matter of public judgment and engagement, which were never

raised in the past. These questions concern the beginning and the end of human life, health care and eugenics, the very definition of humanity, the risks associated with technological advances and their application, and so on. Today, we have to discern how to participate faithfully in the mission of Christ in novel and rapidly changing situations.

An Example: The Beloved Community

The challenge of reading in contexts is daunting, but it is also exhilarating. What would discerning public engagement guided by this kind of reading of the Bible and contemporary contexts look like concretely? Perhaps an example will help, even if it picks out only some of the features of the contemporary situation we have described.

Consider Martin Luther King Jr.'s leadership in the civil rights movement. The core of King's vision of the world was the love of God as revealed in Jesus Christ. "At the heart of our universe," he wrote, "is a higher reality—God and his kingdom of love—to which we must be conformed."[2] The life and death of Jesus show us what that love looks like in action. This love is inherently, unwaveringly forgiving. It is nonviolent. It embraces even the enemy. Love like *that* is at the heart of the universe and was the center of King's faith.

Since King put so much weight on Jesus's commands and example of love, we might expect that he would call for Christians simply to suffer wrongdoings patiently rather than challenging injustice. King certainly did advocate patient endurance, but he denied that patience means inaction. In fact, he believed that you couldn't follow Jesus without seeking to change unjust social conditions. He recognized that "the Christian doctrine of love" must be read in the context of the Hebrew prophetic tradition of denouncing injustice. Jesus said, "Love your enemies and pray for those who persecute you" (Matt. 5:44). Amos said, "Let justice roll down like waters, and righteousness like an ever-flowing stream" (Amos 5:24). King read each in light of the other. The synthesis is stunning in its beauty and power: pursuit of justice that is also the unrelenting quest to convert the oppressor through love. Summarizing his message to his "bitterest opponents," King wrote, "One day we shall win freedom, but not only for ourselves. We shall so appeal to your heart and conscience that we shall win *you* in the process, and our victory will be a double victory."[3]

King wasn't only a great reader of Scripture. He was also a virtuoso at interpreting the contemporary context of mid-twentieth-century America. King understood that the American commitment to democratic sovereignty fundamentally undercut any justification for the systematic exclusion and oppression of a whole group of people and provided a vocabulary in which to express the legitimacy of protest. King also perceived that racism in the United States wasn't a matter exclusively of laws or of economic discrimination or of cultural practices. Rather, all of them were bound up together. Consequently, the civil rights campaigners didn't just campaign for new legislation. They also organized boycotts of discriminatory businesses, and they marched and protested to bring attention to systemic racist practices that prevented Blacks from participating fully in cultural, economic, and political institutions.

In preparing for the marches against segregation in Birmingham, Alabama, in 1963, the Southern Christian Leadership Conference organized training in nonviolence for the marchers. To be permitted to march, each volunteer had to sign a "Commitment Card," promising, among other things, to pray every day, to "meditate daily on the teachings and life of Jesus," and to "walk and talk in the manner of love."[4] The demonstrators understood that public engagement with Jesus Christ as the center and norm calls not only for commitment to following Christ but also for the *formation of a certain kind of character*. In part 3 we'll discuss five of the virtues, or aspects of character, that we need to cultivate if we are to be faithful disciples in our public lives.

Faithful public engagement, however, requires more than just a set of virtues, a Christlike character. Whenever we act in public we are engaged *with something*: a question, an issue, a crisis, a cultural trend. Followers of Christ must reflect on what their faith entails with respect to these particular issues. On rare occasions, the required stance is clear. But most of the issues we commonly face today are ambiguous, as the fervent and protracted debates over them between sincere Christians indicate. In the chapters of part 2, we will identify relevant Christian convictions about pressing public issues of our time and reflect on what these convictions might entail for faithful discipleship in the public square.

Resources for Further Reflection

Introductory Reading

Fowl, Stephen E. *Theological Interpretation of Scripture*. Eugene, OR: Cascade Books, 2009. Fowl offers an accessible introduction to the current movement among theologians to read Scripture theologically with Christ at the center and with attention to the canonical context of the Gospel narratives. The text includes an extended bibliography of books on the subject.

King, Martin Luther, Jr. *A Call to Conscience*. Edited by Clayborne Carson and Kris Shepard. New York: Warner Books, 2001. This volume is a collection of some of King's most momentous public speeches, many of which demonstrate his astute reading of the contemporary American context.

Smith, James K. A. *How (Not) to Be Secular: Reading Charles Taylor*. Grand Rapids: Eerdmans, 2014. Smith offers an accessible summary of the thought of Canadian philosopher Charles Taylor, one of the most perceptive readers of modern Western social and cultural contexts.

Advanced Study

Childs, Brevard. *Biblical Theology of the Old and New Testaments: Theological Reflection on the Christian Bible*. Minneapolis: Fortress, 1993. Childs's monumental work exemplifies biblical theology that attends to each text as a component of the scriptural canon. The book is not oriented toward questions of public engagement in particular.

Gutiérrez, Gustavo. *A Theology of Liberation*. Rev. ed. Maryknoll, NY: Orbis, 1988. This seminal text of Latin American liberation theology exemplifies the practice of thinking theologically about contemporary contexts. Gutiérrez's use of the categories of Marxist social science foregrounds the important question of how theological reflection relates to other disciplines and systems of thought.

Taylor, Charles. *A Secular Age*. Cambridge, MA: Belknap Press of Harvard University Press, 2007. Taylor offers an expansive and challenging interpretation of how "unbelief" became a live option for members of many modern societies and of some of the most significant cultural currents in the world today.

Volf, Miroslav. *Flourishing: Why We Need Religion in a Globalized World*. New Haven: Yale University Press, 2016. Miroslav analyzes some of the key features of the contemporary global context and argues that Christianity and the other world religions have vital resources for shaping globalization processes to serve genuine human flourishing.

PART 2

CONVICTIONS

4

WEALTH

Wealth is a central social good that contributes to human flourishing. We should not define it in narrowly economic terms, and we should not pursue economic wealth at all costs. Economically prosperous societies should worry less about how to create more wealth than about how to create and use the right *kinds* of wealth.

A key component of human flourishing is the enjoyment of created abundance, the astonishing variety of good things, natural and produced, that surrounds us and to which we ourselves belong. Such abundance is the true meaning of "wealth," a meaning much broader and richer than what today generally passes for the wealth of either individuals or nations.

Christianity has had a reputation for despising the world and material abundance. Admittedly, it's not hard to get that impression when St. Anthony (ca. 251–356), a famous desert father and an extreme ascetic, reportedly said, "Hate the world and all that is in it."[1] This saying seems only an intensified echo of the command found in the Bible itself: "Do not love the world or the things in the world" (1 John 2:15). Anthony's way of putting it, however, changed the thrust of that passage, mainly because he altered the meaning of "the world." In John's epistle, it refers to the evil principle corrupting creation; in Anthony's saying, to material creation itself.

The Christian faith ardently affirms the goodness of creation; each aspect of it and all creatures together are good (Gen. 1:31), and it is good to rejoice in creation's goodness (Ps. 104; Isa. 65:18). Correspondingly, the Hebrew Scriptures celebrate the prosperity of the people of Israel, exemplified by an abundant supply of grain, wine, and oil (Deut. 11:13–15). The prophets even make the enjoyment of created goods a central feature of their visions of God's coming eschatological blessing on Israel and the entire planet. Micah proclaims that people from all over the world "shall all sit under their own vines and under their own fig trees" (Mic. 4:4). In Isaiah's description of the new heaven and new earth that God will create, the people "shall build houses and inhabit them; they shall plant vineyards and eat their fruit" (Isa. 65:21).

The New Testament is often thought to be more ascetic than the Old. Taken as a whole, it is not. Jesus didn't go around grimly despising food and drink and merriness. In fact, he was something of a partyer. He went to wedding feasts and even provided an abundance of excellent wine (John 2:1–11). He dined with tax collectors and even Pharisees (Mark 2:14–15; Luke 7:36). He was even accused of being a drunkard (Luke 7:34). In short, he endorsed the goodness of such earthy, material things as bread and wine in the company of friends. What's more, when Jesus described God's kingdom, he often told stories set at parties or relied on the imagery of a plentiful harvest (e.g., Matt. 22:1–14; Mark 4:3–9). Enjoyment of the wealth of creation is part of God's vision for flourishing human life as revealed in the life of Christ.

God intends for human beings to enjoy not only the goods that we simply encounter in the world, like a majestic mountain vista, or those that come directly and miraculously from God, like manna from heaven, but also the fruit of human creativity. That's because God created human beings to be not merely recipients and consumers but also producers and givers. In the second account of creation in Genesis, God plants a garden and puts the first human in it "to till it and keep it" (Gen. 2:15). Adam's role involves a kind of creative activity (cultivating a garden) that derives from and is dependent on God's prior, fundamental creative act (establishing the garden). Human creativity in fact complements God's creativity. God isn't only Adam's benefactor. God and Adam are creative collaborators.[2] Jesus's parable of the talents also suggests the active stance that humans are to take toward the God-given abundance they find in the world. The servants in the story receive the talents in trust from their master, and the master expects them to generate more wealth with the wealth that has been given to them (Matt. 25:14–30).

God created humans (in part!) to enjoy the goods of creation and to participate in the creation of those goods—in a phrase, to create and enjoy wealth. But what is wealth? Not just stuff—whether gold or gadgets, houses or cars—and least of all just money as the means to acquire stuff. Certainly not just possessions—things we can put into our ever-larger "barns" and claim as exclusively ours (Luke 12:18). Wealth is rather all the goods of creation, tangible and intangible, possessed individually or in common. Wealth is scientific discoveries, like the helical structure of DNA or the existence of the Higgs boson. Wealth is water-purification systems that bring safe drinking water to whole cities and countries. Wealth is Bach's *St. John Passion*, Shakespeare's *King Lear*, or U2's *The Joshua Tree*. Wealth is cultures, economic systems, and political societies in which people embrace such a broad notion of wealth and joyfully participate in creating it.

To value wealth is not just to celebrate and enjoy it but also to guard it—to guard ourselves—against its pervasive distortions. Here is a partial list of such distortions:

- *A narrow notion of wealth*. Obsessed as we are with Gross Domestic Product (GDP), we stress the quantity of goods and services expressed in monetary terms while ignoring their nature and quality. Or, thinking that convenience and short-term gain are wealth, we inflict irreparable damage on God's good creation, treating it as mere "raw material" rather than our most important wealth.

- *Mistaken use of wealth*. A good example is so-called positional goods, goods that serve to differentiate us from others and show our superiority to them; we enjoy such goods not so much for themselves as for the relative status they give us.

- *Idolatrous reliance on wealth*. Keenly aware of our creaturely vulnerability, we amass money and possessions in an attempt to secure ourselves against danger; we act as if our salvation comes from Mammon rather than God.

- *Improper acquisition of wealth*. We use oppressive, deceitful, and unjust means to create and acquire wealth.

- *Ascription of ultimate value to wealth*. Forgetting Jesus's commandment to "strive first for the kingdom of God and his righteousness" (Matt. 6:33), we make God a mere instrument for acquisition of wealth.

From this small sampling, we can identify three broad types of distortions of wealth. The first perverts our relation to God. It ranks the possession and enjoyment of created goods over faithfulness to God. It turns the one true God into a mere servant of wealth and turns us into idolaters, worshipers of wealth, which ensnares and enslaves us to it, rather than servants of God, "whose service is perfect freedom."[3] The second type of distortion of wealth denies, implicitly or explicitly, that *all* people are meant to enjoy created abundance. It makes us into the "scoundrels" whom God denounces through the prophet Jeremiah, men and women who "do not judge with justice the cause of the orphan, to make it prosper," but seek instead to enrich themselves at others' expense

(Jer. 5:26–28). The third violates the integrity of our fellow human beings or of creation in general, and it makes us into leeches, who, defying God's vehement condemnation, exploit others (e.g., Deut. 24:14–15; Jer. 22:13) and give no rest to the land so it can be restored (Lev. 25:4–5).

We distort wealth and wealth creation in these ways not only as individuals but also as whole societies. Indeed, to a large extent we do so as individuals because we are part of societies oriented toward inadequate notions of wealth and corrupted forms of wealth creation. Distorted human desires and endeavors, distorted political and economic institutions, and distorted forms of wealth creation all align. Instead of being an expression of our humanity and an enhancement of our lives, wealth and wealth creation are turned into their opposite; distorted ways of creating wealth and enjoying wrongly construed wealth undermine the flourishing of individuals, communities, and their natural habitats.

With this account of wealth creation and its distortion in mind, here are some critical questions to ask about wealth creation in our societies:

- *Is it actual wealth that we are creating?* What passes for wealth in some cases is illusory, no wealth at all. For instance, the bundling of life insurance policies into marketable bonds puts the bonds' buyers and sellers in the position of betting on the deaths of other people and rooting against unforeseen improvements in public health.[4]

- *Are we creating wealth without relying on exploitation or oppression?* Goods that originate in the exploitation of others via unfair wages, harsh labor conditions, and the like are corrupt and corrupting (see chap. 7). Ill-gotten goods may appear to promote the flourishing of those who oppress and exploit. But no one can truly flourish while wronging others.

- *Is wealth creation environmentally sustainable?* Any supposed wealth creation that relies on the unsustainable degradation of the natural environment is actually wealth destruction (see chap. 5). Large swathes of today's economies almost universally fail to pass this test.

- *Do our ways of creating wealth leave space for proper rest?* Given that humans are cocreators with the God who rested on the seventh day, human beings are made not just for creative work but also for celebratory rest (see chap. 7).

- *Are there ample opportunities for all to be involved in creating wealth?* Because we are created to be creators and not just beneficiaries of created abundance, it is important that our societies create wealth without excluding large portions of the population from productive work (see chap. 7).

- *Is the kind of wealth we create broadly accessible so as to potentially help life go well for all people?* Giving more people access to genuine goods is important because God intends for all human beings to enjoy creation.

Room for Debate

Even if we agree to support social arrangements and policies that promote genuine wealth creation, there is still space for legitimate debate among faithful Christians on at least the following questions:

- *What level of material wealth is sufficient for a flourishing human life?* We know that humans need some basic material goods in order to survive, and it's obvious when that need isn't met. It's less obvious when the needed material basis for *flourishing* is or isn't met. It is likely that the answer depends on time and place and therefore needs to be negotiated repeatedly. How we answer this question will have significant ramifications for deciding which public policies are best to pursue.

- *What kinds of wealth contribute to human flourishing?* For instance, what is the relative importance of private and public goods in human flourishing? Is there legitimate room for some "positional goods" that award social status?

- *What particular kinds of wealth should we focus on cultivating and to what extent?* Since we are talking about finite, created goods, there are trade-offs involved in choosing as a society to promote one or another type of wealth. How much should we emphasize artistic goods, knowledge goods, or technological goods, for example? Nothing in the value of wealth creation itself prescribes a particular answer to these questions.

- *Is a particular way of generating wealth acceptable or not?* The debate here is about how the criteria of broadening the access to wealth creation, avoiding exploitation, and so forth apply to a particular case. The complexity of political and economic life will make this in many instances a difficult matter of discernment and public debate.

- *Which policies, institutions, and so on will actually be successful in creating genuine wealth?* This is largely a technical question, but one that is unlikely to be answered definitively through empirical investigation. Consequently, we will have to formulate arguments based on our considered intuitions and best understandings of the available information and then debate which paths are the most likely to promote the good we seek to support.

Resources for Further Reflection

Introductory Reading

Cavanaugh, William T. "Freedom and Unfreedom." In *Being Consumed: Economics and Christian Desire*, 1–32. Grand Rapids: Eerdmans, 2008. Cavanaugh seeks to move beyond debates about the merits of the "free market" and asks instead when a market is free. He argues that true freedom is not the mere absence of constraints but a positive freedom oriented to God. This account of freedom allows us to ask when and how market transactions further or frustrate human flourishing.

Hauerwas, Stanley. "Never Enough: Why Greed Is Still So Deadly." *ABC Religion and Ethics*, October 3, 2011. http://www.abc.net.au /religion/articles/2011/10/03/2922773.htm. Hauerwas claims that we will never be able to recognize our own greed and flourish within limits unless we are formed in a community centered on God's abundance.

Wallis, Jim. *Rediscovering Values: A Guide for Economic and Moral Recovery*. New York: Howard Books, 2011. Written in the wake of the Great Recession, this book argues that economic recovery must include a moral and spiritual reorientation of our values and social policies.

Williams, Rowan. "Trading in the Souls of Men: What Money Can't Buy." *ABC Religion and Ethics*, May 3, 2012. http://www .abc.net.au/religion/articles/2012/04/27/3490873.htm. The former archbishop of Canterbury engages Sandel's *What Money Can't Buy* and Skidelsky and Skidelsky's *How Much Is Enough?* (see "Advanced Study" below) and shows how they both end up gesturing at the need for religion to provide ways of life able to subordinate the pursuit of wealth to human flourishing.

Advanced Study

Alford, Helen, Charles M. A. Clark, S. A. Cortright, and Michael J. Naughton, eds. *Rediscovering Abundance: Interdisciplinary Essays on Wealth, Income, and Their Distribution in the Catholic Social Tradition*. Notre Dame, IN: University of Notre Dame Press, 2006. This collection of essays addresses the theological meaning of wealth and its distribution from the perspective of the Catholic social tradition.

Jackson, Tim. *Prosperity without Growth: Economics for a Finite Planet*. London: Earthscan, 2009. Resulting from Jackson's work as the economics commissioner of the UK's Sustainable Development Commission, this highly accessible book is one of the most important current attempts to develop a macroeconomic vision aimed at both individual flourishing and ecological sustainability.

Sandel, Michael J. *What Money Can't Buy: The Moral Limits of Markets*. New York: Farrar, Straus & Giroux, 2012. This excellent book explores the growth of markets into more and more areas of life and asks us to consider where they are and are not appropriate.

Skidelsky, Robert, and Edward Skidelsky. *How Much Is Enough? Money and the Good Life*. New York: Other Press, 2012. Written by an economist and a philosopher (who are also father and son), this book offers a historical explanation for our current insatiable pursuit of wealth and proposes a secular vision of the good life that tries to answer the question of how much is enough.

Tanner, Kathryn. *Economy of Grace*. Minneapolis: Fortress, 2005. Tanner analyzes Christianity as an economy in which goods circulate according to the logic of God's gracious relations to creation and asks how this vision might impact the contemporary global economy.

5

THE ENVIRONMENT

Human beings, made in the image of God, are part of God's larger creation. Each particular nonhuman creature and all of them together have their own intrinsic value, rather than existing simply for human use and benefit. We must seek to preserve the integrity of creation as an interdependent ecosystem and, if possible, to pass it on improved to future generations. Above all, we should not damage creation by leading acquisitive and wasteful lives.

Recent developments in technology have given humans the power to inflict vastly more harm on Earth's ecosystems than ever before. Deforestation has eliminated up to half of the world's tropical rain forest acreage. Species are going extinct somewhere between one hundred and one thousand times faster than they would without human activities. And human activities have significantly altered the composition of the atmosphere, risking potentially catastrophic changes to the planet's climate.[1] Given the power of technology and the exponential pace of technological advances, the question of how to relate to the planet grows more pressing every day.

The first biblical story of creation has a refrain after each act of creation: "And God saw that it was good" (Gen. 1:10, 12, 18, 21, 25). The light, the earth and the seas, the plants, the sun and moon and stars, the creatures of the sea, the birds of the air, the land animals—all are good. The goodness of creation both precedes and encompasses the goodness of human beings as the creatures made in the image of God. All creation is valuable in its own right, not just for what it can do for humans.[2] Though God's redemption of humanity is at the center of the Christian faith, the rest of creation isn't just the colorful backdrop for the story of redemption. Rather, it *participates* in that story. The non-human creation "was subjected to futility" and groans with labor pains, yearning and hoping to "be set free from its bondage to decay" (Rom. 8:19–22). The reconciling work of God in Christ encompasses "all things, whether on earth or in heaven" (Col. 1:20), which means that humans and the entire ecosystem have been reconciled in Christ. The coming new creation transforms the whole of the creation, not just human beings. That's why so many of the biblical visions of the world to come prominently feature nonhuman creatures. For instance, the prophet Isaiah proclaims that "the wilderness and the dry land shall be glad" and the desert "shall blossom abundantly, and rejoice with joy and singing" (Isa. 35:1–2). All that God made will participate in the everlasting joy of God's kingdom.

This enduring, noninstrumental goodness of creation is the first basic Christian conviction that should shape our engagement with environmental issues. The second is that we humans are *part* of creation. It's common to contrast humans and "the environment" or humans and "nature." But humans are not a different, second creation. We are latecomers on the scene of the *one* creation. Moreover, we are not placed into the creation as alien others but raised up from within it, fashioned from "the dust of the ground," as Genesis 2:7 puts it. The Christian faith affirms that there is one God who created everything else out of nothing. Anything that is, therefore, is either God or a creature. Since we are not God, we are creatures like everything else, and as creatures, we are earthlings, like every other living thing on the planet.

Humans, however, are a special sort of creature, uniquely made in the image of God. We are called into fellowship with God, and just for that reason we are responsible agents within creation. Faced with a situation, we don't just do whatever reflex requires; we are able to actively respond. Humans are also accountable—able to make sense of our actions, to give an account of them, and to be judged for them.

Together, the intrinsic value of creation, our inherent belonging to a world with which together we will one day become the kingdom of peace, and our accountability ground a human responsibility to care for the rest of creation in its goodness. According to Genesis 1, God gave human beings "dominion" over the earth. But dominion is not ownership. The earth is not ours to dispose of as we see fit. To the limited extent that we do own a portion of it, we hold it in sacred trust for the God who made it and loves it.[3]

The second creation story says that "the LORD God took the [first] man and put him in the garden of Eden to till it and keep it" (Gen. 2:15). We can think of tilling and keeping as symbols for two types of responsibility toward the rest of creation. *Tilling* stands for active cultivation of the earth. It signifies intentional human shaping of the natural world. Taken broadly, everything from breeding long-grain rice to making sophisticated nanotechnologies can be seen as part of tilling the earth. In contrast to tilling's active intervention, *keeping* implies looking after the rest of creation, watching over it, and protecting it from harm if need be. These days the rest of creation needs protection mainly from those God has entrusted with protecting it. The charge to keep the garden is thus in great part a charge to stop harming it and instead to align our tilling with the character of the garden and what is growing in it.

Since the nonhuman creation is valuable in its own right, prudent self-interest cannot be the main reason to care for the planet. True, extreme environmental degradation threatens the well-being and survival of humanity. There *are* good prudential reasons to adopt creation-friendly environmental policies and sustainable ways of life. And yet the goodness of the creation that exists now (from marmots to mountains and roses to redwoods) also places demands on our actions. We have a responsibility to preserve the world that we have received, regardless of whether that is necessary for human survival.

Critics have raised a number of objections to making ecological preservation a public priority. None of them is convincing.

Objection 1: Environmental problems aren't that serious, and some, like climate change, aren't even caused by humans.

Reply: Though we have to discern in each case whether a problem is serious, the general claim that environmental problems are trivial is simply not credible. The overwhelming preponderance of evidence suggests that human activity has at least intensified climate change and that without significant action its consequences will be dire.

Objection 2: We don't need to focus on solving environmental problems because when they become serious enough the market will inspire innovative solutions. If the costs of environmental degradation rise enough, it will become profitable to halt and reverse it, and people will think up ways to do so.

Reply: There are two problems with this view. First, it can only apply to protecting *humans* from the costs of environmental degradation. It doesn't take into account the noninstrumental value of the rest of creation. Market mechanisms haven't stopped the extinction of hundreds, and perhaps even tens of thousands(!), of species every year, precisely because humans haven't felt their loss as a cost.[4] Second, it is irresponsible to pass on an incalculable risk to future generations. We just can't be sufficiently confident in the ability of future technologies to halt environmental catastrophes to justify present inaction.

Objection 3: We can deal with the environment once we've lifted everyone out of dire poverty.

Reply: Poverty and environmental degradation are not entirely separate problems; they are bound up together. The poor disproportionately suffer the effects of environmental degradation. They starve when droughts lead to famine, lose water sources when lakes dry up, and perish in the rubble when deforestation causes mudslides. They often live in places where the powerful have expropriated the wealth of the land—whether that be diamonds and gold or fertile soil and abundant fish—and left the weak destitute. Economic plight often forces the poor to degrade their local environments, which then worsens their economic situation. Done rightly, care for the rest of creation can contribute to the flourishing of the poor, not exacerbate their poverty. Moreover, this objection fails to acknowledge the many ways we could dramatically reduce poverty without any per capita economic growth at all and therefore without any additional ecological impact.[5] The math is simple. Current world GDP is over $16,000 per capita.[6] That's $64,000 for a family of four—nothing to scoff at. And yet in 2011, 2.2 billion people were living on less than $2 a day or around $700 a year (less than $8 a day or $2,800 a year for a family of four).[7]

Objection 4: Any society that takes on environmental degradation pays too high a price in economic competitiveness.

Other countries will take advantage of the higher costs of doing business by luring investment and jobs away.

Reply: First of all, it's not clearly established that this is true. For example, political scientist Stephen Meyer has argued that the data point to no significant relationship between state environmental laws and job losses.[8] But more importantly, as Christians, we can't let economic costs deter us from doing what's right. Faithfulness to God is more important than maintaining our current standards of living.

The Big Objection: Objection 3 (poverty) and objection 4 (competitiveness) share an underlying concern about and objection to environmental protection policies—namely, that it's just too *costly* to address environmental degradation.

Reply: The Big Objection makes two mistakes. First, the best information currently available suggests that in the long run, the costs of inaction on climate change will be *much* higher than the costs of action. People in rich countries have effectively been borrowing from the future, living unsustainably and letting the costs accrue to people down the line. The second mistake is to let fear of economic costs trump faithfulness to the God who made and loves the world.

These arguments against putting care for the rest of creation into practice fail. There is no compelling case for continuing to avoid significant action. What, then, should we do? Here are some suggestions:

- *We should lead lives that make good use of the resources of creation and avoid wastefulness.* In modern economies, this will require significant ingenuity and work, but there's plenty that we can do.
- *We should live contentedly and reject the pressure to buy ever-more and ever-newer goods.* Care for the rest of creation

is just one of many reasons Christians should eschew acquisitiveness. We cannot, after all, serve both God and wealth. That our accumulation of things inflicts harm on the nonhuman creation merely adds to the weight of this imperative.

- *We must be faithful in our care for the rest of creation regardless of whether our actions will make a big impact.* We should not underestimate the cumulative effect that many people living eco-friendly lives might have. More importantly, we are called to faithfully witness to God's love displayed in Christ wherever we find ourselves, irrespective of whether we are thereby solving global problems. If the countries in which we live refuse to care for creation, all we can do is care for it ourselves, inspire our friends and neighbors to do so, pray, and trust in God's redemption of the world.

- *Governments should encourage individuals and businesses to adopt environmentally friendly practices and prohibit behaviors that seriously damage creation.* The mix of policies will vary from place to place. A country like the United States should invest in nonpolluting forms of energy, restrict the destruction of natural ecosystems, identify and regulate air and water pollutants, prohibit the killing of endangered species, and so on. All countries should make sure the economic costs of environmental regulations are not borne by their poorest residents.

- *Countries should coordinate a just distribution of the economic costs of halting climate change and other major global environmental problems.* The countries that have benefited the most from the exploitation of the global environment should bear the most cost. But given what we know now about the costs of resource-intensive industrial development, the countries of the Global South would be wrong to claim a right to pollute just as much as the highly industrialized countries did during their periods of industrialization.

- *Trade agreement should hold the partners accountable for environmental impacts.* Global trade shouldn't be a way for corporations to circumvent national environmental regulations.

Room for Debate

- *What are the most important forms of environmental degradation to address immediately?* Given that energy, resources, and political willpower will be limited, what problems are the most pressing? One key factor to consider in these conversations is what damage to creation is irrevocable.
- *To what extent should individuals merely be encouraged to reduce the damage they do to the nonhuman creation, and at what point is legal coercion necessary?*

Resources for Further Reflection

Introductory Reading

Berger, Rose Marie. "For God So Loved the World." *Sojourners*, May 2013. http://sojo.net/magazine/2013/05/god-so-loved -world. Berger shows us both the necessity and the difficulty of responding to climate change and argues that it may take the movement of God in the churches.

Berry, Wendell. "Christianity and the Survival of Creation." *Cross Currents* 43, no. 2 (1993). http://www.crosscurrents.org/berry .htm. Berry reads Scripture while keeping in mind the desirability of the survival of both Christianity and creation and finds much that challenges our common conceptions, not only of nature but also of politics, economics, and labor.

The Evangelical Climate Initiative. "Climate Change: An Evangelical Call to Action." 2006. http://www.npr.org/documents/2006 /feb/evangelical/calltoaction.pdf. This call to action, signed by dozens of evangelical Christian leaders, argues for the reality

of anthropogenic climate change and the moral necessity of
urgent action.

Hamilton, Clive. "The Church and the Ethics of Climate Change."
ABC Religion and Ethics, August 29, 2012. http://www.abc.net
.au/religion/articles/2012/08/29/3578983.htm. Hamilton rejects
the idea that the real problem of climate change is moral complexity; rather, he argues, our moral corruption is allowing us
to undermine commonsense moral solutions.

Advanced Study

Francis, Pope. *Laudato Si'* [Encyclical Letter on Care for Our Common Home]. http://w2.vatican.va/content/francesco/en/encycli
cals/documents/papa-francesco_20150524_enciclica-laudato-si
.html. This groundbreaking papal letter calls Christians to work
toward an "integral ecology" that interweaves care for the environment and care for the poor.

Intergovernmental Panel on Climate Change. *Climate Change 2014:
Synthesis Report*. http://www.ipcc.ch/pdf/assessment-report/ar5
/syr/SYR_AR5_FINAL_full.pdf. This synthesis report presents
the findings of the fifth assessment of the Intergovernmental
Panel on Climate Change, a group of thousands of scientists
tasked by the United Nations with studying climate change.

Jenkins, Willis. *Ecologies of Grace: Environmental Ethics and
Christian Theology*. Oxford: Oxford University Press, 2008.
Jenkins maps three options for a Christian environmental ethic
and insightfully shows that each depends upon a particular
account of the relationship between nature and grace (an "ecology of grace").

McFague, Sallie. *Life Abundant: Rethinking Theology and Economy for a Planet in Peril*. Minneapolis: Fortress, 2001. McFague
tries to teach North American Christians to live differently in
relation to the environment by challenging us to think differently about it.

6

EDUCATION

It is important for all human beings to understand the world in which they live, to learn to reflect critically on the most important question of their lives—namely, what makes life worth living—and to acquire qualifications for jobs that increasingly require complex skills. We should strive for excellent and affordable education for all.

Proverbs 8 portrays personified Wisdom roaming through the land and crying out to all who might listen:

> To you, O people, I call,
>   and my cry is to all that live.
> O simple ones, learn prudence;
>   acquire intelligence, you who lack it.
> Hear, for I will speak noble things,
>   and from my lips will come what is right; . . .
> All the words of my mouth are righteous;
>   there is nothing twisted or crooked in them. . . .
> Take my instruction instead of silver,
>   and knowledge rather than choice gold;

> for wisdom is better than jewels,
>> and all that you may desire cannot compare with
>> her. . . .
> Riches and honor are with me,
>> enduring wealth and prosperity.
> My fruit is better than gold, even fine gold,
>> and my yield than choice silver.
> I walk in the way of righteousness,
>> along the paths of justice,
> endowing with wealth those who love me,
>> and filling their treasuries.
>>> (Prov. 8:4–6, 8, 10–11, 18–21)

We could paraphrase the call of Wisdom by saying that education has two main benefits. First and most importantly, Wisdom teaches "what is right" and leads its students "in the way of righteousness, along the paths of justice." Put in terms of the basic dimensions of flourishing we identified in chapter 2, education equips us to lead our lives well. Second, Wisdom bestows "enduring wealth and prosperity." Its fruit is not shiny metals and glittering stones but honor and prosperity, wealth in the true sense that we discussed in chapter 4. In addition to giving us tools to lead our lives well, education helps our lives go well.

The facets of education that aim most directly at wealth creation are acquisition of knowledge and training in skills. By acquiring knowledge, we grow in understanding of the world. This understanding is itself a form of wealth, and it also contributes to the creation of other forms of wealth, as when a student of chemistry uses her knowledge of the subject to develop a new cancer treatment. Training imparts the specific set of skills necessary to perform a task well. You get trained, for example, to make pancakes in the kitchen of a diner, to operate an MRI machine, or to drive a truck. The skills we acquire through training are often, like knowledge, a form of wealth: it is good to be able to cook a pancake, whether or not you are paid to do so, and even if you rarely do. Of course, exercising such skills is also a means to creating further wealth.

We live in an age of exponentially growing knowledge and stunning technological breakthroughs. Economic success today depends on knowledge and specialized skills. Economic concerns thus drive much of the discussion about education today. As a presidential candidate in 2008, Barack Obama explained his education proposals by noting that "in a world where good jobs can be located anywhere there's an Internet connection . . . the most valuable skill you can sell is your knowledge."[1] On the other side of the American partisan divide, an early version of Wisconsin governor Scott Walker's 2015 state budget proposal included language that removed "the pursuit of truth" from the mission of the University of Wisconsin and added "to meet the state's workforce needs."[2]

It would be a mistake, however, to reduce education to knowledge acquisition and training. Education, as John Henry Newman (1801–90) put it, is "a higher word."[3] The etymology of the Latin word *educatio* suggests rearing or bringing up a child. It isn't so much about acquiring knowledge and skill to succeed in this or that endeavor as it is about cultivating wisdom so as to "succeed" as a human being. Central to this second purpose of education are the formation of character and exploration of the purposes of human life.

Formation of character is the foundation of all education. It embraces the emergence of basic trust in the reliability of the world, emotional development, the nurturing of virtuous habits and dispositions, and so forth. The old phrase for it was the "cultivation of a soul." Done well, character formation requires attachment between student and teacher and a teacher attuned to the particularities of each student. It depends on committed, extended relationships of care and takes place first and foremost in homes.

What sort of character we will seek to form depends largely on the answer to the most important of all questions: Who are we as human beings, and what is the purpose of our existence? To know how to answer these questions well has been the central purpose of education since the founding of modern universities[4] and, indeed, since the dawn of humanity. Historically, reflection on the purposes of human life was undertaken through the study of sacred texts, as was the case in the Jewish tradition to which Jesus belonged (see Deut. 6:6–9). Luke tells the story of the twelve-year-old Jesus, on a yearly visit to the holy city of Jerusalem for the festival of Passover, ditching his family so that he could spend time in God's house, "sitting among the teachers, listening to them and asking them questions" (Luke 2:46). Meditation on sacred texts and questioning engagement with our faith's central stories, rituals, and convictions equip us to wrestle with truth claims about reality and to embrace a vision of the good life for ourselves. With this goal, education is not only good independently of any material benefits it yields; it also helps us assess the value of material benefits and identify possible losses associated with them.[5]

Education is not the same as schooling. Education happens everywhere, at home and on the street, in church and on the internet, at the pub—and also at school. Schooling is one particular way we've gone about organizing education. It involves, roughly, bringing together learners for a designated time, specialized teachers, a curriculum of study, and usually some form of certification for completing a program of study. For most of human history, most people had no schooling at all. It's possible to be wise and to live well without schooling. It's possible to acquire knowledge and technical skills without schooling. Yet in today's complex and rapidly complexifying world, schooling is indispensable, as it gives students access to a much wider array of knowledge and skills than they would have if they were educated only at home or were self-taught.

So far we have discussed how education is good for the people who receive it. But excellent education is good for communities as well. First, the wisdom it imparts can help others lead their lives well. If one person's character is deeply formed in the virtues, she will be better able to support and assist others in living well. Second, much of the wealth that education helps create is public wealth. One person's education helps others' lives go well. The education of the doctors, scientists, and engineers who developed cochlear implants helped bring hearing to hundreds of thousands of people. Third, in democracies at least, an educated citizenry is crucial for the proper functioning of political societies. To undertake any public initiative and to evaluate any public policy or candidate for public office, citizens need to understand both how the world functions and what kind of life, individual and communal, is worth striving for. Because education contributes so much to the flourishing of both individuals and communities, Christians should advocate for universally accessible, excellent education.

We should also be vigilant against the following distortions of education:

- *Reducing the purpose of education to economic growth.* It's a mistake when an individual treats education as merely a means to get into a higher income bracket, and it's a mistake when a country sees its school system as just a tool for growing the national economy and increasing its competitiveness in the world market.

- *Pursuing education to gain social prestige.* The colossal, highly profitable industry and ludicrous expenditure of individual energy dedicated to getting children accepted to the most prestigious universities are evidence of just how much of a hold this distortion of education has on so many people today.

- *Hoarding rather than sharing the benefits of education.* We talk about education as an investment in our own private future. We see it as fundamentally competitive, a zero-sum game in which the neighbor's kids' violin lessons are a threat to my kids' future college prospects and where better science and technology education in China is a loss for Europe, America, and Japan. We fail to perceive that education is a social good, that one of its highest purposes is to equip us to serve others more effectively and more wisely.

Each of these distortions is a matter of cultural values and social structures and not just of individuals' attitudes. To overcome them we need to change individual attitudes, public policies, and social practices.

- *Schooling should not be restricted to acquisition of knowledge and skills but should also include formation of character and reflection on the good life.* In almost every society today, citizens adhere to diverse visions of the good life. Given this pluralism, public educational institutions should not advocate a comprehensive vision of the good life and attempt to shape children in conformity with it. Public schools shouldn't function like monasteries, madrassas, or yeshivas. Still, social pluralism isn't a good reason to confine public education to knowledge acquisition and technical training. Pluralist public schooling can and ought to bring students before the big questions of life and provide resources and skills for reflection on those questions.[6]
- *Schooling ought to be excellent.* It's not enough to just put kids in classrooms. They must receive quality instruction once they're there and the support that leads to actual learning. Teachers should be well trained and well compensated. Schools should be equipped with the tools that best facilitate learning (not necessarily the flashiest new gadgets).
- *Access to excellent education ought to be equitably distributed.* Schools ought to receive the resources they need, regardless of where they're located. Beyond schooling, we should strive for social policies that facilitate excellent education in families and other local communities.

- *Excellent education ought to be affordable.* Globally, cost is a major obstacle to children getting more schooling.[7] Achieving universal access to basic schooling should be a priority of every society. In countries like the United States, where there are (almost) universally accessible public elementary and secondary schools, affordability is an issue primarily for higher education. Between 1984 and 2014, the average real cost of tuition and fees rose by 146 percent for non-profit private colleges and 225 percent for in-state students at public universities.[8]

- *Communities other than schools (families, churches, etc.) are vitally important for excellent education.* If we really value *education* and not just technical training for a productive workforce, we need to support educational communities outside the school system, especially families.

Room for Debate

- *What are the appropriate roles for publicly run schools and private institutions?* Given the importance of universal accessibility, robust public schooling is vital. How extensive it should be and how, if at all, other schools should complement it are open to discussion.

- *At what level of government should public school curricula be set? What degree of commonality should there be between curricula throughout a country?* This is the tension between local control, which is meant to promote flexibility and contextual relevance, and high nationwide standards, which are meant to ensure that the education schools are providing is acceptably excellent.

- *What degree of funding is necessary for an adequate, universally accessible schooling system?* The value of equity should have preeminent bearing on these debates.

Resources for Further Reflection

Introductory Reading

Berry, Wendell. "The Loss of the University." In *Home Economics*, 76–97. New York: North Point, 1995. Schools and universities, Berry argues, are for the making of humanity, a task that requires us to ask and answer difficult questions about what should and should not be learned.

Milbank, John. "Education into Virtue: Against the Tyranny of Modern Mass Education." *ABC Religion and Ethics*, May 9, 2014. http://www.abc.net.au/religion/articles/2014/05/09/400 1516.htm. Milbank argues that modern education has been subordinated to the state; he claims that only through a recognition of transcendence can it educate for something more.

Nussbaum, Martha. "Educating for Profit, Educating for Freedom." *ABC Religion and Ethics*, August 19, 2011. http://www .abc.net.au/religion/articles/2011/08/19/3297258.htm. Nussbaum contends that liberal arts education is crucial to sustaining democratic citizenship and defends this against the growing tendency to measure education by its contribution to economic growth.

Volf, Miroslav. "Life Worth Living: Christian Faith and the Crisis of the University." *ABC Religion and Ethics*, April 30, 2014. http://www.abc.net.au/religion/articles/2014/04/30/3994889 .htm. Miroslav argues that the crisis in higher education stems from the failure to ask what makes a life worth living and proposes that the Christian faith can help revive pursuit of this question.

Advanced Study

Hauerwas, Stanley, and John H. Westerhoff, eds. *Schooling Christians: "Holy Experiments" in American Education*. Grand Rapids: Eerdmans, 1992. This book brings together a diverse collection of theological essays on both public and religious education in America in order to reframe and reinvigorate educational debates.

Kozol, Jonathan. *The Shame of the Nation: The Restoration of Apartheid Schooling in America*. New York: Crown, 2005. This book, which resulted from Kozol's time in dozens of schools across the nation over five years, describes and laments the continuing inequality and segregation of America's schools.

MacIntyre, Alasdair. "The Idea of an Educated Public." In *Education and Values: The Richard Peters Lectures, Delivered at the Institute of Education, University of London, Spring Term, 1985*, 15–36. London: The Institute of Education, University of London, 1987. MacIntyre argues that the two purposes of contemporary education, training people for social and economic functions and producing people who can think for themselves, are irreconcilable without the notion of an educated public as the aim of education.

Mondale, Sarah, and Sarah B. Patton, eds. *School: The Story of American Public Education*. Boston: Beacon, 2001. Based on a PBS series, this highly readable history of American public education provides useful context for current issues and debates.

7

WORK AND REST

Every able person should be engaged in meaningful and, if employed for pay, adequately remunerated work. No one should have to work so unceasingly to meet her basic needs that her life has no room for rest. Both productive work and nonproductive worship of God and enjoyment of created goods are important components of a flourishing human life.

At the end of the sixth day of creation, "God saw everything that he had made, and indeed, it was very good." With the creation of human beings and their placement amid the abundance of the world, "the heavens and the earth were finished, and all their multitude." Hence, "on the seventh day God finished the work that he had done, and he rested on the seventh day from all the work that he had done. So God blessed the seventh day and hallowed it, because on it God rested from all the work that he had done in creation" (Gen. 1:31–2:3).

As Genesis portrays it, God's relation to the world takes two different shapes. There is work: activity aimed at the goal of creating that which is good. And there is rest: celebration and enjoyment of the goodness of what has been created. As is well known, God commanded the people of Israel to commemorate the day of rest that God "hallowed" in the weekly Sabbath. The Sabbath law inscribes the pattern of God's creativity and rest onto the cyclical march of human life. In doing so, it shows something profound about the character of human flourishing. Confronted by legal interpreters in his day who seemed to focus on regulation for regulation's sake, Jesus explains that the work/rest pattern the law prescribes is not some sort of divine whim or annoying imposition: "The sabbath was made for humankind, and not humankind for the sabbath" (Mark 2:27). Like the Sabbath, the six other days too were made for humankind. We flourish when, in an echo of God's work and rest, we too create and celebrate, work and rest. The point is worth emphasizing on both sides.

1. We are meant to *work*. As we discussed in chapter 4, the second creation account underlines the active role of human beings as workers in the garden of creation. Work isn't a consequence of sin; it's part of creation's goodness. Of course, as most of us experience it, work is also toilsome and for some even crushing. That's work marred by sin (see Gen. 3:17). But work itself is good. Working is part of leading our lives well because it helps us create and acquire the means for our lives to go well. Work is thus first and foremost *instrumental* activity. We don't work just for the sake of working; we work to accomplish something (to have a clean home, put food on the table, graduate from college, etc.). And yet we can enjoy work itself, and not just work's results. On a Saturday afternoon, I might take my bike apart, clean and oil it, and put it back together—and enjoy not only the clean and functional bike but also the very activity of making it so. This in fact is the ideal scenario: work as both a means to some goal and a pleasure in its own right. Not all work is like this. If I repair bikes under the tyrannical rule of an exploitative boss, I likely won't delight in it. Indeed, not all work *can* become like this. We cannot imagine, for example, how cleaning an oil spill can be a delight, though it is an immensely important and meaningful

activity. Nevertheless, work at its best is both a means and an end, and as such an expression of our humanity.

Work should not be confused with employment. Employment is an established arrangement by which someone performs a set of duties or completes a set of projects and receives income in return. *Work* is a more encompassing term. We can define work, roughly, as instrumental activity, whether we are remunerated for it or not.[1] It is work in this sense that is part of a flourishing human life. Most employment involves work, but not all work is employment. Caring for a child doesn't cease to be work (not to mention a good bit of toil) just because nobody's paying you to do it. We are meant to work; employment is just one way humans happen to have organized working.

2. We are meant to *rest*. It's important to distinguish between two types of rest: rest as *rejuvenation* and rest as *celebration*. Rest as rejuvenation is what we do to restore the energy that we expend as we go about our lives. For instance, we sleep so that we're no longer tired. Or, usually less successfully, we spend a few hours on the couch watching TV so that we have the energy to manage a household overflowing with chores to be done. Without rejuvenation our bodies and minds break down. But if we take rest to be only rejuvenation, we subordinate it entirely to work. For in an important sense, rejuvenation is part of work—an essential structural element of the "six days" that we are to work. This instrumental picture of rest misses a central feature of rest that the Christian faith has inherited from Judaism: rest as celebration.

We can distinguish two practices involved in celebratory rest, which we'll call worship and feasting. By *worship* we mean time devoted to the praise and adoration of God and to study of the Scriptures. Perhaps it's strange to think of worship as a form of rest, but in the Bible "rest" means cessation of work and striving in particular, not of all activity. By *feasting* we mean time set aside to delight, marvel, and rejoice in the astonishing world God has made, paradigmatically by having a special meal. We see these two practices in Jesus's life. He regularly teaches at synagogue services on the Sabbath (e.g., Luke 4:16; 13:10), and he also attends big celebratory Sabbath meals (Luke 14).

Worship and feasting are both responses to goodness. In worship, we respond in adoration to the unspeakable goodness of God. In feasting, we enjoy the copious goodness of God's creation, which we receive gratefully as a superabundant gift. The traditional center of Christian worship, the Eucharist, brings the two together. We worship God in and by partaking of bread and wine, goods we can enjoy because of both the fecundity of creation and the productivity of human labor.

The idea of celebration underscores that rest isn't primarily a matter of diversion from the hard stuff of life. Rest is more about *immersion*. When we rest well, we become engrossed in the goodness of God and the goodness of all that God has made. Rest as celebration is fundamentally *noninstrumental*. It is an alternative mode of relating to other creatures, to ourselves, and to God. The theologian Jürgen Moltmann remarks about rest:

> With this the view of the world changes: things are no longer valued for their utility and practical value. . . . In pure pleasure, without reason or purpose, things display their creaturely beauty. The world becomes more lovable when we no longer weigh it up according to the criteria of utility and practical value. We shall then also become aware of ourselves—body and soul—as God's creations and as his image on earth. We are then entirely without utility—we are quite useless—but we are wholly there and know ourselves in the splendor of the shining face of God. The fearful questions about the meaning of life and our usefulness vanish: existence itself is good, and to be here is glorious.[2]

In such noninstrumental, immersive, celebratory rest, life being led well, life going well, and life feeling right all align. We rejoice in the goodness of the here and now in anticipation of the joy of the world to come.

Because both work and rest are integral to human flourishing, we should encourage social arrangements that support just and healthy modes and patterns of work and rest.

- *People should have access to employment if they need it.* One of the chief purposes of work is to provide us with the basic requirements of life. It's nearly impossible to make everything you need yourself. To acquire most of those things in modern economies, we need money. Consequently, access to paid employment for those who are able is an important requirement of flourishing. Economic policy ought to prioritize access to employment, possibly even at the expense of higher economic growth.

- *Not just any employment will do.* Work ought to be meaningful, and if possible, it should be enjoyable. There are two problems related to the meaningfulness of work, and they require two different solutions. First, many socially necessary and meaningful jobs are disparaged as insignificant drudgery (think of cleaning and custodial work).[3] We need to elevate the value of these types of employment by raising awareness of their importance and better remunerating them. Second, some jobs really are either morally unacceptable or insufficiently meaningful. Some necessarily distort a genuine good (e.g., prostitution); others may oblige one to commit or support wrong (e.g., soldiering in an army that won't let you decide in which wars you must fight). For still others, the skills they require have been so narrowed that humans doing the work are effectively treated as machines (e.g., repeatedly sewing one small portion of one type of sweatshirt in a factory versus working as an artisan tailor). In all such cases we should endeavor to either eliminate the type of employment or make it more meaningful.

- *Employment should earn workers a fair wage.* This follows from work's purpose of providing the means for survival and flourishing. For people to work and not to be able to obtain those means adequately is a corruption of work. It undercuts work's purpose.

- *We should recognize and value nonemployed work.* The prevalent sense that the level of pay determines the value of a person's work is deeply mistaken. Placing value on creating wealth (in the sense we described it in chap. 4) rather than on making money or increasing economic growth would help, since wealth creation doesn't discount, for instance, care for children simply because it is unpaid.

- *We should ensure that every worker has the opportunity for rest.* Nobody should have to work seven days a week or multiple shifts per day just to put adequate food on the table. All employees should be able to take time away from employment to rejuvenate and to celebrate without risking losing their jobs or not having enough income to survive.

- *We should resist cultural trends that peddle mind-numbing pseudoleisure in place of genuine rest.* Much of the entertainment industry behemoth sells distraction, which at its worst is not even rejuvenating, much less supportive of celebration of God and creation. For those of us accustomed and often even addicted to distraction, genuine rest might feel at first like hard work, but in the long run it will contribute to our flourishing.

Room for Debate

In deliberating about issues of work and rest, the following questions are important topics for debate:

- *What are the required economic, cultural, and political conditions for people to have meaningful work, and who is mainly responsible for creating and maintaining these conditions?* Many of these are empirical questions, but hard ones to get solid answers to. This is an area where it's especially important to pay attention to the constraints that a globalized market economy places on political action. We need to debate not only what should be done but also who can and should do what.

- *How can we best fight unemployment and underemployment?* Given the present state of the economy and future economic developments, how can we stimulate the growth of jobs that pay adequate wages?

- *What kinds of work are meaningful? What kinds are inherently demeaning?* There are bound to be many cases that require careful deliberation and debate. For much of the church's history, being a banker was considered immoral and therefore inherently demeaning. That judgment has changed, and rightly so. But in any given case, we need to be able to articulate why a kind of work is potentially meaningful, or, when the matter calls for it, to make the judgment that a form of labor just can't be good human work. We must not abdicate this responsibility to the market. Just because you *can* make a living doing something doesn't mean anyone *should* make a living doing it.

- *How much time away from work allows people sufficient opportunity to rest? How can we promote a culture that values rest?* These questions are particularly important in the United States, where the average workweek for full-time employees is forty-seven hours, there are zero paid vacation days and holidays guaranteed by law, and over one-quarter of private-sector workers receive no paid time off.[4]

Resources for Further Reflection

Introductory Reading

Berry, Wendell. "Going to Work." In *Citizenship Papers*, 33–41. Washington, DC: Shoemaker & Hoard, 2003. Berry situates work in relation to human needs and local and ecological contexts and in the process offers a sharp theological and philosophical critique of modern "scientific" work.

Jensen, David H. *Responsive Labor: A Theology of Work*. Louisville: Westminster John Knox, 2006. Jensen argues that human work must be understood as a response to the Triune God's work and uses this theological account to present an alternative to the overwork and underemployment of contemporary society.

John Paul II, Pope. *Laborem exercens: On Human Work*. 1981. http://w2.vatican.va/content/john-paul-ii/en/encyclicals/doc uments/hf_jp-ii_enc_14091981_laborem-exercens.html. This important papal encyclical treats labor as the "key to the social question."

Witherington, Ben, III. *Work: A Kingdom Perspective on Labor*. Grand Rapids: Eerdmans, 2011. This accessible book is useful in thinking theologically about one's own approach to labor and employment.

Advanced Study

Hauerwas, Stanley. "Work as Co-Creation: A Critique of a Remarkably Bad Idea." In *In Good Company: The Church as Polis*, 109–24. Notre Dame, IN: University of Notre Dame Press, 1995. Hauerwas offers a theological critique of *Laborem exercens* and presents an alternative vision of the place of work in human life.

Hughes, John. *The End of Work: Theological Critiques of Capitalism*. Malden, MA: Blackwell, 2007. This book critiques the reduction of labor to utility in modern society and offers a vision of labor as participating in God's work.

Meilaender, Gilbert C., ed. *Working: Its Meaning and Its Limits*. Notre Dame, IN: University of Notre Dame Press, 2000. This valuable collection of texts on the significance of work and the importance of rest is drawn primarily from Scripture, theologians, and philosophers.

Volf, Miroslav. *Work in the Spirit: Toward a Theology of Work.*
New York: Oxford University Press, 1991. Miroslav presents
the particular work each of us does as a charism of the Holy
Spirit in light of the new creation and uses this theology to
engage issues of modern labor, including alienation of workers,
unemployment, and environmental degradation.

8

POVERTY

Since God intends for all human beings to enjoy the abundant goodness of creation, God desires that no one live in involuntary poverty. The poor—above all those without adequate food or shelter—should receive special care. A top goal of our public engagement must be to ensure that nobody is condemned to live in abject poverty.

Worldwide, 805 million people don't have enough food to live a healthy life. Vitamin A deficiency alone leads to the deaths of up to 3 million children worldwide every year. Poverty is a global issue, but the poor live even in the richest of countries. Around 45 million Americans live below the poverty line, and 14 percent of American households are food insecure.[1]

In chapter 4 we noted several ways in which sin distorts individuals' and societies' conceptions of wealth and their endeavors to create it. The Bible treats distortions involving abuse of the poor with by far the greatest frequency. For example, God stridently castigates the powerful through the prophet Amos:

Hear this, you that trample on the needy,
    and bring to ruin the poor of the land,
saying, "When will the new moon be over
    so that we may sell grain;
and the sabbath,
    so that we may offer wheat for sale?
We will make the ephah small and the shekel great,
    and practice deceit with false balances,
buying the poor for silver
    and the needy for a pair of sandals,
    and selling the sweepings of the wheat."
The LORD has sworn by the pride of Jacob:
Surely I will never forget any of their deeds.
Shall not the land tremble on this account,
    and everyone mourn who lives in it?

(Amos 8:4–8a)

In another passage some Judeans complain to the Lord, "Why do we fast, but you do not see? Why humble ourselves, but you do not notice?" God replies, "Look, you serve your own interest on your fast day, and oppress all your workers" (Isa. 58:3). The list of passages like these from the Hebrew Bible could go on and on.[2] The point is clear: neglect and oppression of the poor are grave wrongdoings. Indeed, they are an affront to God: "Those who oppress the poor insult their Maker" (Prov. 14:31). Not only is God the maker of all human beings, rich and poor, but God has a special concern for the poor and vulnerable. God is their "refuge" (Ps. 14:6). Their blood is "precious" in God's sight (Ps. 72:14). Their cause is God's cause (Ps. 140:12).

God's special care for the poor reaches its culmination in the incarnation. One defining trait of the gospel is that it is good news *for the poor* (Luke 4:17–20), those whose lives are one instance of bad news after another. When John's disciples ask if Jesus is the Messiah, Jesus points to the evidence: "Go and tell John what you hear and see: the blind receive their sight, the lame walk, the lepers are cleansed, the deaf hear, the dead are raised, and *the poor have good news brought to them*" (Matt. 11:4–5, emphasis added). God's saving work is for all of us, even the rich—though for the rich it entails conversion not just to God but to the poor as well (Mark 10:17–27). God assumed the human nature that we all share—rich, poor, and those in between—but the particular human life God assumed was *not* the life of a king or a wealthy landowner but that of a small-town artisan born into subjection to a foreign empire. It is thus fitting that Jesus equates treatment of the poor with treatment of him: "Just as you did it to one of the least of these . . ." (Matt. 25:40). A beautiful phrase of Pope Benedict XVI sums up well the message of the entire Bible on the matter: the poor of Israel and the poor in general are "God's first love."[3]

The early church was well known for its care of the poor. Some church leaders considered it tantamount to robbery for those with surplus material goods not to give them to the poor. John Chrysostom (ca. 349–407) says, "The rich man is a kind of steward of the money which is owed for distribution to the poor. He is directed to distribute it to his fellow servants who are in want."[4] To refuse to pass on these goods is to seize what is not "destined" to be yours. Basil of Caesarea (329/30–79) vividly draws out the implication.

> When someone strips a man of his clothes we call him a thief. And one who might clothe the naked and does not—should you not be given the same name? The bread in your board belongs to the hungry; the cloak in your wardrobe belongs to the naked; the shoes you let rot belong to the barefoot; the money in your vaults belongs to the destitute. All these you might help and do not—to all these you are doing wrong.[5]

If an individual rich person refusing to give assistance to the needy is a thief, then a society that condones and supports such behavior must be a willing accessory to theft.

The Bible and the entire Christian tradition are clear: without seeking to end involuntary poverty, neither the poor nor the rich can flourish. The first cannot flourish because life cannot go well if we are enslaved to abject poverty, and the second because we cannot lead lives well without alleviating poverty so as to help life go well for others. Less clear, perhaps, is just who "the poor" are and what poverty is. Today, the most common understanding of poverty is extremely low income. According to the World Bank, extreme poverty is an income of $1.25 or less per person per day. As of 2011 over one billion people worldwide qualified.[6] (Think about that for a second. One *billion*: that's the entire population of North America and Western Europe combined.) Defining poverty on the basis of income makes intuitive sense. In modern economies, money gets us access to goods and services, and income is the acquisition of money. And yet focusing just on income is insufficient. We need to expand our understanding of poverty in at least two ways.

First, *assets* are important, not just income. Income is the money you receive from working, gifts, and so forth. Traditionally, your assets are the valuable property you own, such as a house, land, or stocks. Assets like these generate goods you use (a place to stay, crops to eat) or produce financial value that can be converted into income (capital gains on stocks). Similar to assets is human capital, goods like health and intangible resources like technical skills and resilience. Assets and human capital are important because they tend to be more stable than income. They reduce vulnerability to unpredictable circumstance and unjust treatment. If you own your home outright, you can weather a period of low income without becoming homeless. If you can read, it's harder for a corrupt official to take advantage of you. Given that lack of assets and human capital is an important part of poverty, the world today turns out to be even more plagued by poverty than if we looked at income alone. The study of asset poverty is relatively new, and very few reliable statistics on the subject exist, but Credit Suisse's highly conservative estimates suggest that in 2015 over 1.4 billion adults had less than $987 in wealth, with 477 million having less than $132. That figure doesn't include the millions of children in those asset-poor families.[7] Moreover, global asset inequality is even more pronounced than income inequality. The top 1 percent of the world population owned 50 percent of global wealth in 2015, while the bottom 70 percent owned less than 3 percent.[8]

Second, poverty is tied up with *social standing*. Adam Smith (1723–90), the first theorist of capitalism, recognized the cultural dimension of poverty. Distinguishing between necessities ("necessaries") and luxuries, he wrote,

> By necessaries I understand not only the commodities which are indispensably necessary for the support of life, but whatever the custom of the country renders it indecent for creditable people, even of the lowest order, to be without. A linen shirt, for example, is, strictly speaking, not a necessary of life. The Greeks and Romans lived, I suppose, very comfortably though they had no linen. But in the present times, through the greater part of Europe, a creditable day-labourer would be ashamed to appear in public without a linen shirt, the want of which would be supposed to denote that disgraceful degree of poverty which, it is presumed, nobody can well fall into without extreme bad conduct.[9]

As Smith's observation illustrates, the cultural dimension of poverty is intertwined with the material one. The goods we buy and use are loaded with social meaning.[10] And social meanings change as economies and cultures change. Apparently, linen shirts used to indicate that a man met the basic standards of social respectability. Now, they're more likely to suggest trenchant commitment to casualness or exceptional sensitivity to heat. When people point to the high proportion of Americans with poverty-level incomes who own TVs to "prove" that the "supposedly" poor in America have enough money to spend on luxuries, they're ignoring the important social significance of TVs in American life. Whether or not it's a good thing for a society to make owning a TV a prerequisite for social respect, concern for the poor today (in the United States at least) requires acknowledging that it in fact is.

Putting these ideas together, we can see involuntary poverty as *lack of access to the material goods, psychological capacities, basic skills, and social standings necessary for flourishing.* As individuals and societies, we should strive to end such poverty. With this view of poverty in mind, we can highlight some important concerns that should inform our public engagement.

- *A political conversation that focuses almost exclusively on the well-being of the "middle class" is unacceptable.* It's a testament to just how broken much political discourse is today in the United States that poverty receives hardly any attention at all in major campaigns and public debates. Politicians don't think they can get elected unless they convince the majority that their policies will benefit the middle class, which shows that commitment to alleviating poverty isn't important to the middle class.

- *A "trickle-down" approach to addressing poverty is insufficient.* It's not enough to just pursue the goal of economic growth while insisting that it will have the happy side effect of decreasing poverty. What's required is *positive* concern. Attending to the needs of the poor must be a goal in its own right. We need to be able to show that a particular set of policies is most likely to reduce poverty. Sole stress on economic growth does not necessarily lead to poverty reduction. For example, between 1982 and today, the US economy (as measured in real GDP) has grown more than 150 percent,[11] whereas the poverty rate has remained virtually unchanged (15 percent in 1982, 14.5 percent in 2013).[12]

- *Policies and programs to address poverty have to go beyond merely providing increased income.* They must also address the "asset gap" and the social marginalization of the poor. Our public engagement ought to support the building up of relationships of solidarity among all citizens; these relationships are a form of social wealth, and they improve the chances of reducing financial poverty.

- *Focusing on whether the poor "deserve" the care and support of society or trying to distinguish which specific poor people are "deserving" is at best a distraction and at worst a culpable evasion of God's call to combat poverty.* As Chrysostom puts it, "The poor man has one plea, his want and his standing in need: do not require anything else from him; but even if he is the most wicked of all men and is at a loss for his necessary sustenance, let us free him from hunger."[13] Especially in the United States, where the ethic of "personal responsibility" is such a major part of the political culture, supporting the poor irrespective of their deserts can be deeply unsettling. It is, however, what the gospel demands (see Matt. 5:45).

Room for Debate

From a Christian perspective, there is no room for debate about whether our societies should care for the poor. Nevertheless, there are some questions with regard to combating poverty about which Christians can and should debate. Two seem especially significant to us:

- *What are the proper roles of governments, civic organizations, religious communities, and individuals in addressing poverty and caring well for the poor?* There are likely to be complicated trade-offs involved in different ways of distributing the various responsibilities for addressing poverty. How best to answer this question is a matter not just of empirical research but also of practical wisdom.
- *What macroeconomic conditions are most conducive to lifting people out of poverty, and what specific policies are most beneficial to the poor?* Even after we discard a trickle-down

approach, there are still many options, and empirical evidence to decisively identify the most effective among them is lacking.[14]

Resources for Further Reflection

Introductory Reading

Clark, Meghan. "An Option That's Not Optional: The Preferential Option for the Poor." *Catholic Moral Theology*, April 7, 2013. http://catholicmoraltheology.com/an-option-thats-not-optional -the-preferential-option-for-the-poor/. Clark gives a clear and concise explanation of the preferential option for the poor and its significance for Christians. (See also Clark's "Missing the Point on Poverty" on the same site, in which she reminds us that when we talk about poverty, we are talking about real people.)

King, Martin Luther, Jr. "Remaining Awake through a Great Revolution." In *A Testament of Hope: The Essential Writings of Martin Luther King, Jr.*, 268–78. San Francisco: Harper & Row, 1986. In this sermon, the last of his life, King confronts America with its obligation to use its abundant wealth to truly address poverty.

Milbank, John. "The Poor Are Us: Poverty and Mutual Fairness." *ABC Religion and Ethics*, November 23, 2010. http://www .abc.net.au/religion/articles/2010/11/22/3073193.htm. Milbank draws on the Christian tradition to challenge a widespread assumption of both the right and the left: the poor are not us.

Smiley, Tavis, and Cornel West. *The Rich and the Rest of Us: A Poverty Manifesto*. New York: Smiley Books, 2012. This treasure trove of stories and information about contemporary poverty also proposes twelve "poverty-changing ideas."

Advanced Study

Bailey, James P. *Rethinking Poverty: Income, Assets, and the Catholic Social Justice Tradition*. Notre Dame, IN: University of

Notre Dame Press, 2010. Drawing from Catholic social teaching, the capabilities approach to development, and recent social science, Bailey argues that poverty can be combated much more effectively in an asset paradigm than an income paradigm.

Bounds, Elizabeth M., Pamela K. Brubaker, and Mary E. Hobgood. *Welfare Policy: Feminist Critiques*. Cleveland: Pilgrim, 1999. This highly relevant resource for thinking about the impact of welfare policies on poverty also considers the relation of these policies to larger economic trends.

Sobrino, Jon. *The Eye of the Needle: No Salvation outside the Poor: A Prophetic-Utopian Essay*. London: Darton, Longman & Todd, 2008. Sobrino, a Latin American theologian targeted for assassination because of his commitment to the poor, offers a radical critique of the economic and political order from the perspective of the poor. He argues that there can be no social or historical salvation without receiving a new way of life from the poor.

United States Catholic Bishops. "Economic Justice for All: Pastoral Letter on Catholic Social Teaching and the U.S. Economy." November 1986. http://www.usccb.org/upload/economic_justice _for_all.pdf. The US bishops assert that the economy must serve the ends of human dignity, especially for the poor, and that this includes basic economic rights such as material sufficiency, employment, and medical care.

9

BORROWING AND LENDING

As individuals and as a nation, we should live within our means and not borrow beyond what we can reasonably expect to return, and when we are able, we should lend generously, responsibly, and fairly. We shouldn't off-load onto others, whether our contemporaries or future generations, the price of our over-reaching or risk taking; neither should we seek to profit from others' misfortunes or to prioritize our financial gain over the needs of others. We should save so as to be able to give to others who are less fortunate than we are.

Many of us use credit cards for everyday purchases without even thinking that we are technically borrowing money when we do so. Of the thousands of Americans who bought a new car between April and June 2013, 84.5 percent relied on some sort of financing.[1] Presumably most of the rest, who paid "cash," withdrew the funds from a bank account of one kind or another. As these examples illustrate, modern life and modern economies would be unthinkable without lending and borrowing. Though many current forms of lending and borrowing seem almost natural to us, they are in fact changing inventions. They have been designed and practiced in ways that are both beneficial (strengthening social ties and generating wealth) and deeply flawed (exploiting the weak and ruining entire communities). Our main concerns here will be the distortions of lending and borrowing that pervert debt from an instrument for promoting human flourishing into a source of misery and ruin.

1. *Distorted lending.* There are numerous commandments in Scripture meant to curb distortions of lending. The law prohibits taking interest on loans from one Israelite to another (Deut. 23:19), and it requires the cancellation of debts every seven years (Deut. 15:1). In the New Testament, Jesus says, "Give to everyone who begs from you, and do not refuse anyone who wants to borrow from you" (Matt. 5:42) and "Love your enemies, do good, and lend, expecting nothing in return" (Luke 6:35a). Commands of this sort are apt to strike modern readers as radical and unrealistic. But a deep theological reason, illumined by the parable of the unforgiving servant (Matt. 18:23–35), undergirds them.[2] We all are debtors before a generous God. When we're harsh toward our debtors, we fail to emulate God's generosity toward us. Exodus gives the same rationale for its laws about debt slavery: since God delivered the Israelites from debt slavery in Egypt, they must not just turn around and use debt to enslave their neighbors.[3]

Building on these scriptural sources, Christian thinkers through the centuries condemned usury, abusive lending. Early on, some considered it wrong to take any interest at all. Over time, a near consensus developed that lending with interest can be permissible and even good if it contributes to the generation of wealth. Still, most theologians and church bodies left significant restrictions on lending in place. They all agreed on one thing, however: lending becomes distorted when it's aimed at personal profit without regard to the flourishing of the borrower or the community as a whole and especially when lenders take advantage of the poor. A general rule of thumb is this: *lending should never be practiced in a way likely to harm the borrower.*

Harm can mean that debt makes the borrower's life *go* exceedingly poorly. To repay a debt, for example, she is forced to choose between having the heat shut off and going further into debt. Or a poor country's debt obligations leave it without funds for education, pensions, or basic infrastructure. Harm can also mean that a debt makes it difficult for a borrower to *lead* his life well. He is, for example, permanently exhausted because he works more than he should to pay off the debt and is therefore cruel to his children; he cuts corners wherever possible to make an extra buck and is incapable of being generous with time or money. Or the offer of seemingly boundless credit lures borrowers to spend excessively on luxury goods for personal comfort and social prestige, buying bigger houses, nicer cars, and more elaborate plastic surgeries than we can actually afford.

To say that the type of lending practiced shouldn't make it unduly hard for the borrower to lead her life well isn't to deny the responsibility of the borrower. Borrowing responsibly rather than self-indulgently is in fact part of leading life well. It draws attention to an aspect of Jesus's teaching that those of us living in atomized societies tend to forget—namely, that we are responsible not just for ourselves but for one another. "If any of you put a stumbling block before one of these little ones who believe in me, it would be better for you if a great millstone were fastened around your neck and you were drowned in the depth of the sea. Woe to the world because of stumbling blocks! Occasions for stumbling are bound to come, but woe to the one by whom the stumbling block comes!" (Matt. 18:6–7).

2. *Distorted borrowing.* Borrowing is distorted when it is done for the sake of superfluous consumption rather than for productive investment or to meet basic needs. The social good of borrowing is that it facilitates wealth creation of the kind we discussed in

chapter 4. Going into debt to buy unnecessary consumer products doesn't generate true wealth, even if it allows the engine of economic growth to keep on churning, running on fumes. Granted, it is not easy to determine what superfluous goods are, and it ought to be left to individuals to decide. But a good example might be so-called positional goods—goods we value in great part because others don't have them. A standard Apple Watch currently costs $349—not an affordable watch by any means. A functionally equivalent and otherwise identical Apple Watch *Edition* with an eighteen-karat-gold body costs $10,000. That's a positional good, designed exclusively to set its wearer apart from others. If we're spending our way deeper into debt, buying goods that serve mainly to show off our wealth and importance, we're using deceitful means to demonstrate a hollow pretense of social superiority and spurring our neighbors to do the same.

Borrowing is also distorted when it is unsustainable. Such borrowing habituates us in dishonesty and borders on theft. We pretend to others, and often to ourselves, that we will be able to cover the cost when payment is due. (In cases where unsustainable borrowing results from desperate needs, the distortion is not so much on the side of the borrower as on the side of a society that fails to address her needs by any means other than unsustainable lending.) At the national level, unsustainable borrowing amounts to sacrificing our children's and grandchildren's well-being to the idol of our present comfort, since they will be faced with the choice of paying back with interest every dollar we borrow or defaulting on the national debt and suffering as a consequence.

Unproductive and unsustainable borrowing prevents us from living generously. The psalmist explicitly contrasts people who borrow wrongly and those who give well: "The wicked borrow, and do not pay back, but the righteous are generous and keep giving" (Ps. 37:21). A flourishing human life involves sharing with others out of our abundance or, if times are tight, out of whatever little we have. (Recall the widow's mite [Mark 12:41–44].)

Accruing nonproductive debt or borrowing unsustainably obligates us often to pay so much to lenders that it robs us of freedom to participate in the generous circulation of goods to which God calls us.

What are some political implications of this vision of generous, responsible, and fair lending and borrowing?

- *Lending to those in poverty or acute financial need at high interest rates with crushing fees is abhorrent, and we ought to eliminate the practice.* There are over twenty thousand payday lenders in the United States lending billions of dollars to low-income borrowers, often at annual rates over 320 percent.[4] It is wrong to profit at the expense of the poor. In 2013 more than 11 million Americans had to take on high-interest credit card debt to pay medical bills, and over 1.7 million lived in households going through bankruptcy due to medical debt.[5] It is wrong to force those made vulnerable by illness or accident to borrow unsustainably. Some will argue that payday loans provide a needed service without which the borrowers would be worse off and that putting medical bills on a credit card is better than not receiving care or going bankrupt straightaway. That might be true about the way things are today, but a Christian commitment both to care for the poor and the sick (see chaps. 8 and 12) and to generous, responsible, and fair lending demands that we seek alternatives. When it comes to meeting people's basic needs, giving should take priority over lending.

- *We should seriously consider debt relief or forgiveness for low-income countries and individuals with unbearable debt burdens.* When debt has come to harm the borrower, its terms should be revisited. The imperatives to care for the poor and promote human flourishing will in some cases require sacrificing lenders' returns.

- *Ever-increasing national debt with no realistic prospects for surpluses in the future is irresponsible.* At some point, every political society has to pay the costs for its public services. That means aligning tax levels and service levels in the long run. Refusing to do so foists the costs of our comfort on future generations.

Room for Debate

Within the framework of good lending and borrowing, there are at least four areas for significant debate:

- *What are responsible levels and kinds of debt for households, businesses, and nations?* At what point does borrowing become unsustainable? What conditions justify adding debt?
- *What exactly are predatory lending practices, and what is the best approach to preventing them?* At issue here is precisely how much risk of harm to borrowers is acceptable.
- *How much debt spending for the sake of economic stimulus is acceptable, and what should that spending go toward?* Endeavors to stimulate growth in times of recession often rely on intentional government deficits, whether from tax cuts or spending initiatives. It is a matter of debate how much debt is too much to take on to increase GDP and, perhaps more importantly, what it should finance.
- *When is it appropriate to focus public policy on reducing debt?* The question is not only what fiscal policy is most conducive to growing GDP and/or bringing down national debt. We must also wrestle with the possibility that GDP growth cannot be increased without irresponsible or unfair debt practices. And there is the further question of when it is right to take measures to discourage, for example, further credit card or educational debt.

Resources for Further Reflection

Introductory Reading

Bretherton, Luke. "Neither a Borrower nor a Lender Be? Scripture, Usury and the Call for Responsible Lending," *Christian Ethics Today* 21 (2013): 3–7. http://christianethicstoday.com/wp /wp-content/uploads/2013/12/final-fall-edition-ce91.pdf. Bretherton discusses usury in Scripture and the theological tradition and highlights the ways borrowing and lending can both build up and tear down interdependence, cooperation, and mutual responsibility.

Kuttner, Robert. "The Debt We Shouldn't Pay." *New York Review of Books*, May 9, 2011. http://www.nybooks.com/articles /archives/2013/may/09/debt-we-shouldnt-pay/. This insightful article uses a discussion of David Graeber's landmark book, *Debt: The First 5,000 Years* (Brooklyn, NY: Melville House, 2012), to address political and moral questions surrounding bankruptcy and debt relief.

McCarthy, David Matzko. "Debts and Gifts." In *The Good Life: Genuine Christianity for the Middle Class*, 104–7. Grand Rapids: Brazos, 2004. McCarthy offers a short reflection on personal debt and the use of monetary resources drawing from the parable of the talents.

Welby, Justin. "Payday Loans: Archbishop's Speech in the House of Lords." June 20, 2013. http://www.archbishopofcanterbury .org/articles.php/5083/payday-loans-archbishops-speech-in-the -house-of-lords. Justin Welby, archbishop of Canterbury, raises moral questions about payday lending and charts a course for the church to create an alternative.

Advanced Study

Bretherton, Luke. "'Love Your Enemies': Usury, Citizenship, and the Friend-Enemy Distinction." *Modern Theology* 37 (2011):

366–94. Drawing from scriptural and historical sources, Bretherton interprets usury, the act of lending with interest, as a political act that requires theological assessment in light of Jesus's command to love one's enemies.

Hyman, Louis. *Borrow: The American Way of Debt; How Personal Credit Created the American Middle Class and Almost Bankrupted the Nation.* New York: Vintage, 2012. This fascinating history of debt in America demonstrates both the promise and the peril of modern practices of lending and borrowing.

Veerkamp, Ton. "Judeo-Christian Tradition on Debt: Political, Not Just Ethical." *Ethics and International Affairs* 21 (2007): 167–88. Veerkamp develops insights into contemporary problems surrounding debt from both the law and the political practice of the Hebrew Scriptures.

10

MARRIAGE AND FAMILY

Though subordinate in value to singleness for the purposes of the gospel, marriage and family serve important social goods. They embody enduring covenantal commitments and are indispensable for raising children. The state should support marriages in which children are raised and should accord equal legal treatment to other-sex and same-sex marriages.

Christian reflection on marriage and the family has to wrestle with the relationship between two important convictions that stand in tension with each other. The tension forms the backdrop for our main topic here, which is not so much the Christian stance toward marriage and family in general as responsible Christian *public engagement* with regard to marriage and family.

On the one hand, the New Testament questions the importance of marriage and family. Jesus calls people out of their families (Matt. 4:21–22; 19:29; 23:9). He considers those who do the will of his Father in heaven closer kin than his own mother and siblings (Matt. 12:46–50). He says that he has "come to set a man against his father, and a daughter against her mother, and a daughter-in-law against her mother-in-law" (Matt. 10:35). He chastises those who let family obligations hold them back from following the call of the gospel (Matt. 8:21–22). In a similar vein, the apostle Paul laments the divided interests and anxiety about "the affairs of the world" that come with marriage (1 Cor. 7:32–34). For both Paul and Jesus, singleness is preferable to marriage. Paul counsels the Corinthians to remain unmarried if they can (1 Cor. 7:8–9, 25–40). And Jesus praises those "who have made themselves eunuchs for the sake of the kingdom of heaven" (Matt. 19:12). Whatever else Christians say about the importance of marriage and the family, we can't lose sight of these significant caveats.

On the other hand, while Christian faith relativizes marriage and family, it also affirms that they are oriented toward genuine and fundamental goods. One is the raising of children. The stable, loving bonds that families ought to provide are vital for the formation of children's basic trust in the world. Families are also central sites for the passing on of vital cultural traditions and for moral and religious instruction (Deut. 11:18–19), for learning by close observation and shared practice what the good life is and how to live it. In a phrase, families are meant to be cradles of flourishing human lives. Families should (and often do) support the formation of flourishing people; marriage in turn should (and often does) found stable, nourishing families.

The stress here is on the *rearing* of children, not the begetting of them, to use a stereotypically biblical word. Marriage in particular isn't necessary for the sheer making of humans. Indeed, sometimes marriage hinders it, as in cases of infertility. Marriage and the families it can ground are more pivotal for the *raising* of humans. Joseph, for instance, is clearly superfluous to the holy family as far as procreation goes, and yet in Matthew the contribution that his marriage to Mary makes in Jesus's life is palpable (Matt. 2:13–23). It would be presumptuous to say that the family is the *only* social form capable of raising flourishing children, but it is an institution uniquely well suited for this purpose. Other social forms of child rearing succeed to the extent that they become family-like by promoting the goods that properly functioning families provide.

It is noteworthy that Genesis doesn't tie the origin of marriage directly to the command to be fruitful and multiply but notes along with the command only the creation of humans as male and female (Gen. 1:27–28). The scriptural story of marriage begins with God's observation, "It is not good that the man should be alone," and the subsequent creation of one who is for the first human "bone of my bones and flesh of my flesh" (Gen. 2:18, 23). This points to a second reason Christians should affirm the importance of marriage: it demands and nurtures deep covenantal commitments that both instantiate and foster human flourishing. Such commitments, increasingly rare in contemporary societies dominated by short-term, renegotiable, contractual relations of mutual convenience, reflect in a human way God's unconditional and abiding love, the foundation of the divine covenant with humanity. This is why the Christian tradition, following Jesus's teaching, has historically insisted on the indissolubility of marriage. It is also why Christians can see marriage as a reflection (or sacrament) of the relationship between Christ and the church (Eph. 5:22–33). Marriage is not a contract of convenience but a lifelong covenant of human beings with the most intimate and abiding of ties. Christians, obviously, often do not live up to this ideal. Still, abiding and unconditional love is what we sign on for when we enter the marriage bond.

Like all social institutions, the family and marriage are historically changing realities. They undergo transformations over time. We see a shift already in the Bible. Abraham and Solomon were not the kind of husbands an early Christian overseer was supposed to be, "the husband of one wife" (1 Tim. 3:2 KJV). The independent nuclear family of today's increasingly global middle class is significantly different from the Roman household of Cornelius the centurion (Acts 10). The romantic marriage between true loves that contemporary Westerners idealize and project onto Robin Hood and Maid Marian is a far cry from the experience of most actual medieval Britons. These transformations don't mean that we're left without biblical and theological handholds for thinking about marriage and the family today, but they do require care in how we reason from the past to the present; we should not presume that we know just what it means to say something like "marriage is part of the order of creation."

What implications do the historical transformations of marriage and family and a Christian account of them have for judgments on those matters in contemporary politics? Many governments actively support marriage in ways they do not support singleness. Since marriage as such is neither necessary for human flourishing nor normative, the presumption should be that government not privilege marriage over singleness in the absence of further reasons to do so. Raising children is different. Other than strong families, there is no viable way that we know of to provide for the rearing of every child in a society. Families, then, are necessary for flourishing. The government therefore has a responsibility to lend active support to those raising children, whether that support comes through tax policy, mandatory paid parental leave, or other approaches.

At the forefront of public debates in many countries today is the question of same-sex marriages. The best first step with a subject as controversial as this is to make sure we actually have the *question* right. We need to distinguish between three different sets of issues that often get confused. There's the question of whether churches should bless any same-sex unions and, if so, which ones and with what relation to the marriage blessing. Call this the *ecclesial* question. Then there's the question of whether enduring covenantal relationships between people of the same sex should receive the same treatment under the law as analogous relationships between people of different sexes. Call this the *legal* question. Neither the ecclesial nor the legal question is the same as the *moral* question about what kind of sex between whom is licit. This moral question certainly has a lot of bearing on how we might answer the other questions, especially the ecclesial one, but it doesn't *entirely determine* how we must do so.

Roughly, we can think of the ecclesial and legal questions as forming a matrix with two variables, meaning that there are four logically possible positions.

1. *Positive/positive.* The church should bless same-sex unions, and governments should treat same-sex and different-sex covenants the same.

2. *Negative/negative.* The church should not bless same-sex unions, and governments should give different or no legal standing to them.

3. *Positive/negative.* The church should bless same-sex unions, but governments have good reason not to treat same-sex and different-sex covenants the same.

4. *Negative/positive.* The church should (continue to) withhold its blessing on same-sex unions, but governments should treat same-sex and different-sex covenants the same.

There are more or less plausible and recognizably Christian arguments for each of these four possibilities. Since our concern in this book is the common good in pluralistic societies and not the communal morality of the followers of Christ, we'll appeal to the churches to debate the ecclesial and moral questions with love, patience, and the minimum possible rending of the body of Christ, and we'll focus our discussion on the legal question.

It is our judgment that Christians should support providing the same set of legal protections and provisions to same-sex as to other-sex unions. We recognize that in saying this we put ourselves in opposition to the basically unanimous stance of the Christian tradition for most of its history (though, of course, the distinction between aspired communal morality and public legislation is relatively recent). Until the last several decades, in every place where the government has regulated marriage the church has either tacitly or vocally supported the exclusion of same-sex unions from the same set of legal protections as other-sex unions. To explain why we depart from this tradition, we'll present what philosophers call an a fortiori argument. We'll make the case that Christians have good reason to support the legal equality of same-sex and other-sex unions even when they consider sex between people of the same sex inherently illicit. If that's the case, then surely if we come to a different moral judgment about same-sex relations, the reasons to support legal equality will only be stronger.

The basic idea is this: both of the reasons for the importance of marriage—founding stable families for the rearing of children and forming deep covenantal commitments—are applicable to same-sex unions. Governments thus have just as much reason to actively support and/or to remove obstacles to same-sex covenantal unions as they do for other-sex unions, and it would be unjust not to equally support them without good reason. But why should that be the case if, as many Christians believe, sex between people of the same sex is inherently illicit? Well, the goods of rearing flourishing children and of covenantal communion could exist despite what are deemed to be sinful sexual practices. These goods are not necessarily a consequence of sex, even if they are de facto inextricably bound up with it in nearly all marriages. Indeed, this is just a variation on how all goods exist in the fallen world. These goods might be imperfect, only haltingly achieved, and in some ways at odds with themselves, but that doesn't take away their goodness. Worshiping a God who specializes in creative, redemptive interaction with broken creatures and their broken goods, all Christians can affirm that genuine goods worth legally supporting come out of same-sex unions, even if they consider the sex involved in these marriages to be inherently illicit. If this line of thinking holds up, then even Christians who hold to traditional moral evaluations of sex between people of the same sex can see support for the legal equality of same-sex unions as part of faithful public discipleship in support of the goods of marriage and the family.

Room for Debate

- *What policies are required to support strong families?* How can these policies be shaped so that they give support to both two-parent and other family arrangements, such as when grandparents or other relatives are the primary guardians and caregivers of children?

- *Should the set of legal protections and provisions relating to unions between couples be called marriage?* Might there be reasons for the state to get out of the marriage business? Is there any justification for using different words for the same legal provisions when they apply to same-sex couples rather than other-sex couples?

Resources for Further Reflection

Introductory Reading

Johnson, Luke Timothy. "Homosexuality and the Church: Scripture and Experience." *Commonweal*, June 11, 2007. https://www.commonwealmagazine.org/homosexuality-church-1. In this article, Johnson argues that while the church cannot affirm homosexual sex based on the New Testament text, it can and should affirm those same-sex loving relationships that demonstrate holiness. Johnson argues that the Christian engagement on the topic of same-sex relationships has to go beyond the mere text of Scripture, just as it has, he argues, on topics such as slavery.

Wright, N. T. "Humanum 2014." Humanum video, 16:36. Posted November 18, 2014. https://www.youtube.com/watch?v=AsB-JDsOTwE. Wright argues that the difficulties of the Christian account of marriage described in the New Testament are to be celebrated rather than jettisoned as they stand as a reminder of the difficulties of the relationship between Christ and his church, of which marriage is an analogy.

Advanced Study

Forsyth, Andrew. "Defining Marriage." *Soundings: An Interdisciplinary Journal* 97 (2014): 297–322. Forsyth carefully responds to influential arguments for a definition of marriage centered on procreation set out by Robert P. George, Sherif Griggs, and Ryan T. Anderson.

Rubio, Julie Hanlon. *A Christian Theology of Marriage and Family*. Mahwah, NJ: Paulist Press, 2003. Working from a postmodern Catholic perspective, Rubio deprioritizes the centrality of marriage and the family in favor of the normative relationship of "small Christian community." She argues that the notion of a nuclear family generates a political dilemma between obligations to "family" and obligations to "outside" that the small Christian community avoids.

Williams, Rowan. "The Body's Grace." *ABC Religion and Ethics*, August 24, 2011. http://www.abc.net.au/religion/articles/2011 /08/24/3301238.htm. Williams argues that reproductive sex is not a norm of the biblical sexual ethic. Using the idea that sexual metaphors are central to the Bible's discussion of the relationship between God and God's people, Williams argues instead for other norms—for example, vulnerability—that begin to capture the complexity of this relationship.

11
NEW LIFE

Unborn human life, just like fully developed human life, deserves our respect, protection, and nurture; consequently, we have a responsibility to care in special ways for those who bear new human life into the world.[1]

Human life is precious. God creates human beings out of love and for love, loving them into an inestimable worth. Human beings are not valuable merely as an aggregate or a species. *Every* human life is precious. All of us individually are precious not on account of any capacity we have or excellence we have achieved, but for the sheer fact that God is attached to each one of us, without any merit of our own. Affirmation of the singular value of every particular human life is central to the Christian faith. It informs the convictions expressed in many chapters of this book, and it is the lodestar for navigating the turbulent moral and political waters that churn around the life gradually developing in mothers' wombs.

We have stated the conviction at the beginning of this chapter in terms of *"unborn* human life." In doing so, we implied that birth is not the relevant point at which to distinguish what is human life from what isn't. That is not to say that a newborn isn't significantly distinct from a "newone," as ethicist James Mumford has called the unborn.[2] Plenty of things change at birth. Perhaps most relevantly, although a newborn is still totally dependent on others for survival, the little one is no longer dependent *on one particular other* in the exclusive way a newone depends on the pregnant mother. The period of what is commonly called "viability" designates the time during which the newone is still *actually* exclusively dependent on the pregnant mother but likely *could* not be. Assuming that infanticide is morally repugnant, the (befuddlingly indeterminate) beginning of viability marks the *latest* conceivable point in pregnancy at which the newone must be considered an unborn *human* life and thus be accorded the respect, protection, and nurture a human life deserves. In "Room for Debate" below, we will note the debate about whether we should treat the beginning of viability as the decisive point. For now, we can think through the value of unborn human life while leaving open precisely when human life begins.

The value of unborn human life is a special instance of the value of human life in general. The imperative to care for unborn human life, in turn, is a special instance of the imperative to care for human life in general. In this special case, the imperative has two sides: care for the newone and care for the pregnant woman.

With respect to care for the pregnant woman, it's important to affirm two things at once. First, bearing a newone does *not* reduce a woman to a mere incubator and transporter of a future baby. She is important as a human being in her own right. Second, a pregnant woman is unlike other human beings precisely because she is pregnant; the newone in her womb *adds* to the ways in which we have obligations to care for her. Special forms of care include the following:

- *Expanded health care.* Pregnancy is not itself a "medical condition," even if insurance companies say it is. Nevertheless, from the early days through delivery, pregnancy does bring heightened risk of certain health problems and involves significant changes in a woman's body. It is crucial, therefore, that pregnant women have access to affordable care from medical specialists.

- *Education.* Health care that helps pregnant women navigate the normal physiological changes of pregnancy should be part of a broader system of educational resources for them and their close relations (especially expecting fathers).

- *Economic protection and support.* Women should not be economically disadvantaged because they are pregnant. Those who are employed should not lose their jobs or suffer reduced pay if the effects of pregnancy interfere with their ability to perform the tasks of their usual jobs. Pregnant women and expecting fathers also ought to be able to look forward to guaranteed paid leave and (as in Singapore and Finland) receive economic support to help absorb the initial shock of the costs of raising a child.[3]

- *Expanded social support.* Relationships of emotional and practical support are crucial to a flourishing pregnancy, not to mention parenthood. Policy and social norms ought to push prospective fathers to be supportive, rather than fleeing the responsibility that they have taken on themselves. And we should seek ways of providing support to pregnant women whose close relations have not supported them.

Turning now to the care that we ought to give newones themselves, the first thing to note is how vulnerable they are. They cannot move themselves to avoid dangers. Neither can they cry out for help. They are especially susceptible to harm from environmental threats (tobacco smoke, air and water pollutants, etc.). There is almost no sense in which they can be expected to protect themselves, so others must protect them. Protection is not, however, the only form of care that unborn human lives deserve. Specific forms of care include the following:

- *Prenatal and perinatal health care.* The medical attention involved in caring for a newone will usually overlap almost entirely with those involved in caring for her pregnant bearer, but the newone is a developing human life in her own right. Offering adequate health care for newones is a matter not only of protecting them from harm but also of nurturing them so that they can flourish. It thus involves ensuring the provision of good nutrition and making necessary intrauterine medical interventions accessible and affordable.
- *A safe environment.* Newones ought to be protected from exposure to environmental pollutants like mercury, lead, and tobacco smoke and from poisons taken in by their mothers, such as alcohol and prescription or illicit drugs.
- *Preparing a home.* Caring for a newone entails providing the conditions for her future flourishing. Perhaps most importantly, that means preparing a welcoming home for her when she makes the transition from newone to newborn. We use "home" here in a broad sense, including the whole physical and social environment into which the child will be born. Thus, for example, making quality child care accessible and affordable for families where all the present parents need to work is part of preparing a home.

So far, we have been discussing the two sides to the one imperative to care that follow from the value of unborn human life, care for the newone and for the pregnant mother. In most cases, these are reinforcing imperatives. But since pregnant women deserve care in their own right, not only on account of carrying a newone, the possibility of competition does exist. Most definitely, this is the case when continuing a pregnancy would involve severe risk to the life of the pregnant woman. More controversially, there are situations in which pregnant women experience a stark tension between the demands of their own good and the demands of caring for a newone.

This is where the question of abortion comes into the picture. Put somewhat abstractly, that question is: What, if any, are the situations in which some other concern (most especially, care for the prospective mother or worries about the newone's prospective quality of life) trumps the imperative to care for the newone such that it is justifiable to take steps that will result in the end of the newone's existence?

A strong case can be made that abortion is justifiable when the mother's life is at serious risk. While there is no greater love than to be willing to die for another, the Christian tradition has wisely refrained from claiming that such self-sacrifice should be legally enforced. A great many Christian thinkers have even declined to say that it is morally obligated. In many other cases of apparent conflict between care for the pregnant mother and care for the child in her womb, abortion is clearly unjustifiable. In still other cases, there is perplexing ambiguity and, as we'll discuss below, legitimate debate. As a general rule, it is wrong to privilege the woman's sense of what care for her entails at the expense of the continued existence of the newone. This is especially true once the newone is an unborn *human* life. The immeasurable value of each human life and the obligation to care especially for the most vulnerable demand such a stance.

Poor communal support exacerbates and in some cases entirely creates many situations in which women experience a strong conflict between care for themselves and care for a newone and decide in favor of abortion. The primary goal of the totality of policies, social arrangements, and cultural attitudes relating to pregnancy and abortion should be to maximize the alignment of care for pregnant women and new mothers and care for newones and newborns. Adoption is a particularly good way to secure such alignment. We should seek to make the path of giving children for adoption easy for pregnant women and new mothers who choose it. Even under the best of circumstances, bringing a child into the world will cause a woman significant inconvenience, but it should never be economically and socially unbearable.

Questions about the *legality* of abortion must be considered in the context of the moral ends that we ought to seek—namely, the reduction of abortions and the fostering of care for both newones and pregnant women. Even those who rightly oppose unjust abortion laws need to discern how much of their finite resources they should dedicate to active opposition to those laws and how much to other measures. The primary concrete implication of the value of unborn human life for faithful Christian public engagement with the issue of abortion is: *We ought to advocate for measures that effectively reduce the number of abortions.* Why care about reducing abortions regardless of when during pregnancy they occur? For one thing, the complexity of the debate and lack of consensus about when human life begins should make us extraordinarily cautious. But even were we to come to the conclusion that unborn *human* life begins well after conception, we shouldn't presume that a developing newone that is not yet a human life would be owed no protection at all. So the chief criterion here is what achieves the moral goal of fewer abortions. If a specific set of social policies, like those that alleviate poverty, reduce the number of abortions, that's an argument in their favor. If a certain sort of sex education does, it should be seriously considered. If widely available, subsidized family planning services effectively reduce the number of abortions, they should be implemented.[4] And so on.

Room for Debate

The past several decades of controversy over abortion in the United States underscore that this area calls more urgently than

most for the virtues we discuss in chapters 21 through 25. We
need courage, humility, justice, respect, and compassion if we're
going to engage these controversies faithfully. The judgments in
question are vexingly difficult. It should come as no surprise that
the debates will be too. One thing should remain uncontestable:
an unborn human is a precious human life and is all the more
precious for its utter vulnerability. Still, there *are* difficult questions here, and there are places where debate is not only legitimate
but necessary.

- *What type of countervailing concerns can justify abortion?*
  Debate here will have to address such anguishing cases as
  pregnancies resulting from rape and incest.
- *What counts as "unborn human life"?* The Catholic hierarchy, among others, has famously stated that life begins
  at conception.[5] Historically, however, it is not a unanimous
  judgment of Christian thinkers that *human* life is present
  from the moment of conception.[6] Christians must wrestle
  with the best scientific data available to them, reading these
  data through theological lenses and doing their best to judge
  accordingly. One relevant scientific finding available today
  is the observation that "around half of all fertilized eggs
  die and are lost (aborted) spontaneously."[7] Does this tell us
  something about when human life begins, or is it instead
  a tragic loss of unborn human lives that results from living in a fallen natural order? Another relevant issue is the
  shifting point of viability. Are embryos becoming human
  several weeks earlier than they used to thanks to advances
  in medical technology?
- *What would be the moral status of a developing newone
  who is not yet an unborn human life?* This question would
  have significant bearing on the judgments we should make
  about how to weigh care for the pregnant woman and care
  for the newone during this period.

Resources for Further Reflection

Introductory Reading

Kaveny, Cathleen, and Marie Griffith. "Roe v. Wade at 40: An Interview with Legal Scholar and Theologian Cathleen Kaveny." *Religion and Politics*, January 23, 2013. http://religionandpolitics
.org/2013/01/23/roe-v-wade-at-40-an-interview-with-legal-scho
lar-and-theologian-cathleen-kaveny/. In this interview, Kaveny
discusses the meaning of *Row v. Wade* after forty years and how
she attempts to be pro-life without engaging in the culture wars.

Meilaender, Gilbert. "Abortion." In *Bioethics: A Primer for Christians*, 25–37. Grand Rapids: Eerdmans, 1996. Meilaender argues
that Christians must reject the individualism and the idea that
personhood depends on capacity that often underlie support
for abortion.

O'Brien, Dennis, Peter Steinfels, and Cathleen Kaveny. "Can We
Talk about Abortion?" *Commonweal*, September 12, 2011.
https://www.commonwealmagazine.org/can-we-talk-about
-abortion. This valuable exchange between three Catholic thinkers addresses the permissibility of abortion and the difficulty
of addressing it in public discussion.

Advanced Study

Anscombe, G. E. M. *Human Life, Action, and Ethics*: *Essays by
G. E. M. Anscombe*. Edited by Mary Geach and Luke Gormally.
Charlottesville, VA: Imprint Academic, 2005. The first part of
this collection ("Human Life") contains a rich and challenging
set of essays on the value and meaning of human life, especially
at its beginning.

Cahill, Lisa Sowle. "Reproduction and Early Life." In *Theological
Bioethics: Participation, Justice, and Change*, 169–210. Washington, DC: Georgetown University Press, 2005. Cahill aims
to give due consideration to all the values in play in decisions

surrounding the unborn and asks what kinds of social solidarity and community are necessary to minimize the need to sacrifice one value for another.

Hauerwas, Stanley. "Abortion: Theologically Understood." In *The Hauerwas Reader*, edited by John Berkman and Michael Cartwright, 603–22. Durham, NC: Duke University Press, 2001. Hauerwas argues that Christians ought to leave behind the language of rights and personhood in their approach to abortion and develop a more theological and ecclesial approach.

Mumford, James. *Ethics at the Beginning of Life: A Phenomenological Critique*. Oxford: Oxford University Press, 2013. Mumford challenges the idea that opposition to abortion is only possible on religious grounds by drawing on the philosophical tradition of phenomenology.

12

HEALTH AND SICKNESS

All people—poor or rich—should have access to healthy living conditions and affordable basic health care, two things that are essential for our lives going well. Each person is responsible for living in a way conducive to physical and mental health; that's part of leading our lives well.

In 2013 the United States spent 17.4 percent of its gross domestic product on health care, up from 13.4 percent in 2000. That's over nine thousand dollars per person, and it doesn't include the billions of dollars spent on health that don't go to medical care—spending for things like multivitamins, gym memberships, and herbal supplements. An estimated 1.7 million Americans suffered through bankruptcy because of high medical bills in 2013. Around 80 million people skipped needed medical care because of the cost. And even with all that spending, Americans aren't especially healthy. A 2013 report found that against sixteen similarly wealthy nations, the United States ranked fourth-worst in death from communicable diseases, third-worst in death from cardiovascular disease, and worst in death from congenital anomalies and in overall mortality.

The United States consistently ranks at or near the bottom among its peer nations in infant mortality and life expectancy.[1]

Compared with most of the world, however, the US health-care system is downright luxurious and phenomenally successful. Worldwide, there were about 198 million cases of malaria in 2013. According to UNICEF, about one in nine children born in Africa will die before turning five. Relatively basic medical care could prevent many of those deaths, but low-income countries have only 2.8 doctors per 10,000 people, compared to 28.6 per 10,000 for high-income countries. Clean drinking water and sanitation systems could save many lives, but today 783 million people don't have access to clean water, and 1 billion people across the world practice open defecation.[2]

Health is a significant part of life going well; attending to our own and our neighbors' health is therefore part of leading our lives well. Jesus's ministry illustrates both points. Jesus himself cared intensely for others' health. He healed the sick at almost every turn, from Simon Peter's mother-in-law (Mark 1:29–31) to the slave of the high priest (Luke 22:50–51). The Gospels connect these healings with Jesus's mission of bringing the kingdom of God: "Jesus went throughout Galilee, teaching in their synagogues and proclaiming the good news of the kingdom and curing every disease and every sickness among the people" (Matt. 4:23; cf. Matt. 9:35). When God's reign comes, sickness is overcome. People are made well. That's why we too are called to care for the health of our neighbors. It's also why we have a responsibility to care for our own health. Living in ways that recklessly tear down our own health treats God's good gift carelessly. Christian public engagement with national and global health should reflect these convictions.

As Satan in the story of Job knew, our health tends to concern us more deeply than anything else does. Just for that reason, care for health—our own and that of others—easily gets distorted. As we engage in public debates about health, we should keep an eye out for these warped forms of care for health. Three types of distortions are especially significant today.

First, we turn *care* for health into *obsession* with it. We arrange our lives and world largely to maximize our health. Food and exercise start to lose meaning other than their contribution to our health. Appeal to health becomes a trump card in many arguments. Such obsession has the acrid smell of idolatry to it. Focused on our own health, we forget that life is more than health food and the body more than a slender waistline, and we fail to "strive first for the kingdom of God" (Matt. 6:33).

As with all idolatries, worship of health leads to bondage (see Gal. 4:8; 5:1). Slaves to the ideal of a "healthy lifestyle," we are unable to put it aside if necessary for the sake of a greater good. Moreover, obsession with health is in some regards like works righteousness: it never achieves perfection but often results in arrogance. Obsessed with the health of the body, we become sick in the soul. We then look down on the unhealthy with the prim eye of the Pharisee from Jesus's parable: "God, I thank you," we pray, "that I am not like other people: slackers, smokers, overeaters, or even like this slob. I exercise four times a week; I pay a tenth of all my income for yoga classes and organic superfoods." This is no less sin than being careless about our health. And like carelessness about health, obsession with it has political consequences.

If we think of illness predominantly as the deserved consequences of a moral failure, we're likely to begrudge medical care to those who need it. Why should *we* have to pay higher insurance premiums so that *they* can get help when their irresponsible behavior finally catches up with them? The question is not illegitimate, but it twists the appropriate and important impulse to encourage people to be responsible about their health into self-righteous and judgmental disregard for our neighbors' actual well-being. It ignores the complex causes of poor health and disease, and it fails to care for our neighbors as whole human beings who are cross-pressured in many ways, subject to forces outside their control and, yes, morally imperfect. None of this makes them less worthy of medical care.

Second, we care for our own health but not for our neighbors'. This distortion emerges in numerous forms. Most egregious is the stark inequality in access to basic medical care, both globally and within countries like the United States. In Chad, around 20 percent of children die before the age of five. Across Europe, that number is 1.3 percent.[3] According to a 2013 Centers for Disease Control study, in the United States, 37 percent of the poor and 30.5 percent of the nearly poor didn't have health insurance between 2008 and 2010, compared to 8.9 percent of the nonpoor.[4] Not to address this is to act like the Levite and priest in the story of the good Samaritan. It is an outrage that we leave so many uncared for or bankrupted by the cost of medical treatment. Adding to the scandal is the way the wealthy spend more and more extravagant sums on less and less necessary and helpful treatments. According to the American Society of Plastic Surgeons, in 2010 Americans spent over $10 billion on cosmetic plastic surgery procedures.[5] Meanwhile, worldwide, only $2 billion was devoted to malaria control.[6]

Caring for our neighbors' health isn't just a matter of access to affordable health care. It is also a matter of healthy living and working conditions. Nearly 8 percent of children in the United States from families with incomes below the poverty line live within one mile of an environmental hazard site.[7] The US Department of Agriculture has estimated that more than 23 million Americans live in food deserts—that is, towns and neighborhoods where people lack "ready access to fresh, healthy, and affordable food."[8] Conditions like these contribute to disease and bad health and make it virtually impossible to live in ways conducive to health. So do working conditions that poison or break down the worker's body. And so do wages and work hours that keep people from being able to exercise or eat well. Caring for the health of our neighbors in obedience to Christ demands that we work to address such damaging conditions.[9] For members of one segment of a community to expend time and resources to perfect their health while others are practically doomed to ill health is wrong.

Both obsession with health and failure to care well for our neighbors' health are connected to a third distortion of care for health: we treat health care as a commodity. The goodness of things like plates and pencils is almost completely unaffected if they are bought and sold as commodities. Other goods, like friendship, are almost completely eviscerated if we treat them as commodities. Still others sit somewhere in between; treating them as commodities doesn't totally disfigure them, but it doesn't leave them untouched either.[10] Health care is this third sort of good. In a society where health care is treated as a commodity, you can still get your appendix out (although it might cost you an arm and a leg). Yet a genuine good is lost if patients become customers first and foremost. Their individual stories and worries and well-being then matter only if they contribute to "efficient" or profitable transactions. Add to this the fact that, in the words of Dr. Paul Farmer, "the commodification of medicine invariably punishes the vulnerable," and it becomes clear how treating health care as a commodity seriously distorts genuine care for health.[11]

If we are committed to loving care for our neighbors' health and responsible care for our own, we won't just seek to avoid distortions of health care, however. We will also undertake positive steps to improve it. Here are a few ideas to get the conversation started:

- *Public health measures that give people the opportunity to live healthy lives must be adequately funded.* Such measures range from lead abatement and cleaning up toxic waste to providing free antimalaria bed nets in the Global South,[12] from regulating the food industry (sugar!) to supporting community gardens and ensuring access to fresh and healthy foods in urban environments.

- *A top priority of health-care systems should be ensuring that everyone has access to affordable basic care.* The intuition that we should be able to use our money to buy better versions of things and services than others can afford is deeply ingrained and widespread. I shouldn't be kept from buying a $400,000 house, this intuition says, just because there are people who can't afford the same. Limiting the health-care advantages money can buy for the sake of ensuring affordable basic care for all feels oppressive. But privileging the right to buy your way to exclusive health care at the expense of universal access to basic care goes against the gospel principle of care for our poor neighbors' health.

- *Institutions and policies related to medical research should promote progress in combating health problems that primarily affect the poor.* For-profit medical research tends to focus predictably on the potentially most profitable problems, which are often those most affecting the affluent. Diseases like malaria, which primarily afflict people too poor to pay for premium drugs, receive comparatively little attention. Since the lives of the poor matter as much as the lives of the rich—since they are "God's first love"—it is imperative to correct this imbalance.

Room for Debate

- *What are the best ways to ensure access to affordable basic health care?* What are the proper roles of government, businesses, nonprofit organizations, and churches in providing access to health care?

- *How should public health initiatives be prioritized?* In most cases, the question will be not whether to leave a problem completely unaddressed but rather what level of resources should be committed to it at any given time. Still, thinking in terms of setting priorities provides guidance for the inevitable tough decisions.

Resources for Further Reflection

Introductory Reading

Berry, Wendell. "Health Is Membership." In *Another Turn of the Crank*, 86–109. Washington, DC: Counterpoint, 1995. Challenging the assumption that health is primarily about the individual, Berry points to a communal and nondualistic vision of health that would serve to reorient the modern health-care industry.

Gawande, Atul. "Overkill." *New Yorker*, May 11, 2015. http://www.newyorker.com/magazine/2015/05/11/overkill-atul-gawande. This fascinating article chronicles the problem of unnecessary care and the way it can crowd out necessary care in the American health-care system; it also highlights promising approaches to the problem.

Kaveny, Cathleen. "Commodifying the Polyvalent Good of Health Care." *Journal of Medicine and Philosophy* 24 (1999): 207–23. Kaveny considers the goods of health care and asks how they are distorted when commodified in a market system.

Kenny, Nuala P. "The Good of Health Care: Justice and Health Reform." *Health Care Ethics USA* 19 (2011): 2–8. https://www.chausa.org/docs/default-source/general-files/the-good-of-health-care---justice-and-health-reform-pdf. This article argues that markets in health care are not always neutral and can often distort the good of health as part of the common good.

Advanced Study

Cahill, Lisa Sowle. "National and International Health Access Reform." *Theological Bioethics: Participation, Justice, and*

Change, 131–68. Washington, DC: Georgetown University Press, 2005. This chapter, written prior to the Affordable Care Act, critically evaluates the problems and prospects of health care in America and around the world. Cahill then asks how a "participatory" theological bioethics can contribute to reform.

Farmer, Paul. *Pathologies of Power: Health, Human Rights, and the New War on the Poor.* Berkeley: University of California Press, 2005. This important book draws on Farmer's extensive experience as a physician in Haiti and calls for a new liberation theology–inflected paradigm in thinking about health and human rights.

Hauerwas, Stanley. "Salvation and Health: Why Medicine Needs the Church." In *The Hauerwas Reader*, edited by John Berkman and Michael Cartwright, 539–55. Durham, NC: Duke University Press, 2001. The real question of health care, Hauerwas contends, is not how we can relentlessly pursue cures for all diseases but rather what kind of communities we need in order to sustain the long-term care of the ill.

Townes, Emilie M. *Breaking the Fine Rain of Death: African American Health Issues and a Womanist Ethic of Care.* New York: Continuum, 1998. Townes develops an ethic of care through lament of the current state of health care in America, particularly in African American communities; attention to issues of race, gender, and class makes this especially illuminating.

13

AGING LIFE

> Those who are frail on account of their advanced age deserve our special care. They need adequate medical assistance, social interaction, and meaningful activities. The humanity of a society is perhaps measured especially by how it treats those no longer capable of doing "useful" work.

Every human life is precious and consequently deserves our care, we said in chapter 11. We should not, as Friedrich Nietzsche thought, care exclusively for the highest peak of human development and disregard the mass of "common natures," to say nothing of "the downtrodden, the miserable, the malformed, the failures."[1] The most vulnerable ought to receive special forms of care attuned to the specific needs of each. These basic Christian convictions apply to the elderly as well, especially in fast-paced, future-oriented societies that place a high premium on self-sufficiency and economic utility.

In Shakespeare's *As You Like It*, Jacques draws a quite graphic analogy between old age and the weakness and inability of infancy. In the life of a human being, he says, the "last scene of all, that ends this strange eventful history, is second childishness and mere oblivion, sans teeth, sans eyes, sans taste, sans everything."[2] This is likely an exaggerated picture of what old age holds for most of us. And yet it does vividly evoke one of the most characteristic features of aging: the progressive loss of capacities we once took for granted. This waning of powers is what makes special care for the elderly necessary.

Where once we could climb mountains, now the three stairs to the front door count as a hike. Where once we could keep a whole grocery list in mind and recite whole poems from memory, now the night of oblivion swallows even the phone conversation that happened five minutes ago. Where once we could provide for many of our own needs through work and employment, in old age self-sufficiency diminishes. A construction worker can no longer swing a hammer or operate a backhoe. An executive's body can no longer handle the wear and tear of a hectic travel schedule, and her wits can no longer keep pace in the boardroom. Such productivity slips irrecoverably out of reach. Diminished bodily and mental capacities increase a person's vulnerability and thus add to the forms of care she needs and therefore ought to receive.

The same reason that care of elderly people is necessary—their diminished capacities—is also the reason that some people think we should be sparing in giving it. When elderly people cease to be able to perform economically productive work, it is no longer possible to explain their continuing preciousness in terms of their economic contribution to us or to society. Some therefore conclude that continued expenditure of energies and means for ongoing care for them are no longer justified. Whereas we might rely on economic interests to justify care for and nurturing of children—"I will not be alone in my old age!" or "They are the workforce of tomorrow!"—the productivity of the elderly who can no longer work is all behind them. As old age advances, our "usefulness" to society tends to decline in proportion to the resources we need, often to the point that by a coldly utilitarian calculus we become a "net negative" for society.

Tying care to utility is profoundly mistaken. First, many elderly people with no economic utility still have important goods to give. The proverbial "wisdom of old age" is proverbial for a reason, even if in fast-changing societies we value it less than we used to do. More significant than the gifts some elderly are able to give are the gifts that all elderly themselves are. Each human being is a gift merely by being who she is, an elderly person with extremely diminished capacities included. Moreover, precisely in their infirmity, elderly people are living reminders of the inescapable fragility and finitude of our lives. In contemporary societies we push fragility and finitude out of sight and out of mind—often living in denial of the true nature of our humanity and losing the capacity for genuine empathy.

Second, responsibility to care for each human being is in fact never grounded primarily in his actual or potential productivity. Recall that human life is not defined by productivity (chap. 7). We are called both to work and to rest. Humans don't cease to be valuable and worthy of care when the six days of their work lives are done and the closing years of their lives are spent in Sabbath rest. Care is not primarily an investment. Neither is it primarily a reward or recompense for services rendered. In fact, care is predicated not on anything a person *does* but on what each person *is*. The root of people's value is the elemental fact that they are God's, that God loves them and is attached to them. And that's also the reason for our care, generous rather than utilitarian in nature.

As individuals and communities, we are called to care for the elderly and do so in specific ways that correspond to the character of their needs. Public debates today tend to focus on the need of the elderly for income and medical care. Both of these are legitimate and pressing needs. Those who are unable to be employed should not live in poverty or go without basic health care. Even if they may be deficient in some ways, social insurance programs for the elderly (Social Security and Medicare in the United States) are admirable ways to care for the elderly on an immense scale. Yet even the best of such programs would not be sufficient on their own, since care for the elderly entails more than attending to their economic and medical needs and vulnerabilities.

In cultures where meaning and work have become closely bound together and where work is associated mainly with employment, the unproductivity of retirement can lead to existential crisis. A life without work seems to be a life without purpose. Effective care for the elderly requires providing opportunities for meaningful activities and helping them enjoy the goodness of ordinary life. It also entails that we recognize the agency of the elderly, refraining in all but the most extreme cases of incapacity from treating them as mere recipients of care.

Human beings are profoundly social creatures. To flourish we need many kinds of relationships with other people. But especially in societies dominated by fast-moving market economies, the process of aging threatens to strip people of these relationships. Peers pass away, at first slowly but then with alarming frequency. Children are apt to move away or become focused on managing their own households and careers. Old work relationships often fade in the years following retirement.

Most all of us will undergo at least two deaths. There is biological death, when the complex systems of our bodies disintegrate and cease to sustain us as living beings. There is also *social* death, when the relationships that partially constitute our lives gradually wither away, and we fade from the consciousness of those whom we have loved and are eventually forgotten. To care for the elderly well is to ensure that *social death does not occur before biological death*. We ought to nourish cultures and build societies that do not let the elderly experience the sorrow of social death while their bodies still live.

Given the vulnerabilities and needs of the elderly, here are some ways to make our care concrete:

- *We should ensure that the systems we set up to provide financial resources and health care for the elderly are well funded and reasonably easy to navigate.* Social insurance for the elderly that is constantly at risk of running out of funds hardly counts as insurance. Programs that provide only a small fraction of the income one needs to live on risk leaving elderly citizens in abject poverty. In the United States, the percentage of citizens over the age of sixty-five who are poor has fallen from 28.5 percent in 1966 to 9.1 percent in 2012.[3] We should celebrate such progress and build on it. We should resist the tendency to treat the elderly as "freeloaders"; doing so is a testimony to our own lack of human kindness.

- *We should encourage our fellow citizens to care for the elderly whom they know and to reach out to those who have been left alone.* Part of being a responsible citizen is participating in a culture of comprehensive care for the elderly. We should support ways to engage children and youth with the elderly.

Room for Debate

Questions we should carefully weigh in making judgments about how to care for the elderly include the following:

- *At what point is the expenditure of resources required to extend and improve the lives of older citizens simply too high?* The fact that each person is precious means that *all* are precious. We are to care for all, and therefore, given limited resources, we will need to make hard decisions about when care for some must receive fewer resources so that care for all can continue. The physiological end of life is not the worst thing that can happen to someone. The desperate attempt to hang on to physiological life at any cost is mistaken (see chap. 14). At some point trying to extend or improve life must give way to acceptance of biological death and preparation for it. Debate should be about not whether but when this shift should occur.

- *To what extent should government institutions help provide noneconomic and nonmedical forms of care for those who are left alone?* A number of complicated questions are involved here. How best can we ensure that all the elderly receive these forms of care? Are governments capable of providing it? Would government involvement send the implicit message that citizens have no individual responsibility to care relationally for the elderly? How might governments support individuals who undertake the long-term care of elderly citizens?

- *What are the responsibilities of nonstate communities toward the elderly?* How can and should religious institutions, businesses, and other communities contribute to care for the elderly? How should they participate in economic and medical support? To what extent should they serve as substitutes for state-provided services?

Resources for Further Reflection

Introductory Reading

Conference of European Churches. "Ageing and Care for the Elderly." June 2007. http://csc.ceceurope.org/fileadmin/filer/csc/Ethics_Biotechnology/AgeingandCareElderly.pdf. This document draws on Christian ethical convictions to criticize the value placed on youth and argues for dignity and respect for the elderly.

General Council of the United Church of Canada. "An Ethical and Theological Statement on Aging." August 2000. http://www.united-church.ca/allages/seniors/ouch/ethical. This document puts aging in a theological context in order to draw ethical and political implications for church and society.

Advanced Study

Cahill, Lisa Sowle. "Decline and Dying: Cultural and Theological Interpretations." In *Theological Bioethics: Participation, Justice, and Change*, 70–101. Washington, DC: Georgetown University Press, 2005. Cahill discusses the underlying cultural context of aging and death in our society in order to shed light on ethical decisions surrounding the end of life.

Harris, J. Gordon. *Biblical Perspectives on Aging: God and the Elderly*. Philadelphia: Fortress, 1987. This book provides a careful and detailed analysis of scriptural perspectives on aging and the elderly.

Hauerwas, Stanley, Carole Baily Stoneking, Keith G. Meador, and David Cloutier, eds. *Growing Old in Christ*. Grand Rapids: Eerdmans, 2003. This collection challenges contemporary visions of aging in light of a scriptural and theological vision.

Moses, Sarah M. *Ethics and the Elderly: The Challenge of Long-Term Care*. Maryknoll, NY: Orbis, 2015. Moses insightfully presents the contemporary social and ethical challenges around aging and the elderly and offers a theological vision to guide Christian response.

14

ENDING LIFE

Life is a gift—mostly a beautiful gift, but sometimes an almost unbearably burdensome gift. The beginning of our life is not in our hands; the end of life should not be in our hands either. This is the dignity of our vulnerable lives: we are not our own but belong to the God of love, who created us, redeemed us, and will bring our lives to fulfillment.

Advances in public health and medical technology have led to growing elderly populations and more medical treatment for those nearing death.[1] They have also increased our ability to keep terminally ill people alive for prolonged periods of time without restoring them to full health and functioning. How should we treat life with diminished capacities in light of increased ability to delay death's arrival? Two widespread options are physician-assisted suicide and euthanasia. These procedures are currently legal in five countries and three US states. A California woman received national media attention when she moved to Oregon, where assisted suicide is legal, and publicly announced the date she would end her life weeks in advance.[2] Should the terminally ill, especially those living in excruciating pain or with radically diminished capacities, be permitted to schedule their own deaths? Do we have the right to bring about our own death?

The cost of medical treatment in the last years of a person's life can be crushing. For 40 percent of households of Medicare recipients, the out-of-pocket medical expenses in the last five years of life exceed the household's financial assets.[3] Should delaying death for terminally ill or severely incapacitated people put their families in debt or bankrupt the health-care system? Death raises important political questions, not only existential ones.

As the cessation of existence, death is an evil; as the end of biological life as we know it, death is part of that life itself. We are born, we mature, and when we have grown old and "full of years," we die, as the Bible says of Abraham (Gen. 25:8). Similarly, the aged and righteous Simeon saw his death not as a tragic cessation of life but as the appropriate end of his lifelong service to God: "Master, now you are dismissing your servant in peace, according to your word; for my eyes have seen your salvation" (Luke 2:29–30). Still, we mourn—not so much the reality of dying as the departure of the loved one. It is different when death comes prematurely, taking away a child, for instance, cutting her life short, unlived. In the Gospels, it wasn't good for Jairus's "little daughter" or Jesus's young friend Lazarus to have died; Jesus raised both from the dead. But even when life seems interrupted, death is not the worst thing that can happen to a human being. Biological death can't be the greatest evil because biological life isn't the highest good. If it were, martyrdom wouldn't make sense. The martyr recognizes the truth to which the fear of death blinds us: it is worse to betray your deepest commitments by denying Christ than it is to die. There is a deeper life that gives meaning and direction to biological life; to save that life, Jesus's disciples might need to lose their biological lives (Luke 9:24).

Though not the *highest* good, ordinary human life is *a precious and inviolable good*. God gives life to human beings and brings it to fulfillment, and God loves each life with a value-bestowing love of unbreakable attachment.[4] Intentionally destroying a human life is a great evil. Imagine someone were to break into the Accademia di Belle Arti in Florence with a sledgehammer and pound Michelangelo's *David* into dust and rubble. Imagine taking a child's beloved teddy bear—the one with an eye missing and stuffing falling out—and capriciously throwing it into the flames. Deliberately taking a human life is akin to wantonly destroying a prized possession, whether that is a sculptural masterpiece or a battered toy, except in this case God is the one who loves and seeks communion with what has been destroyed. That's why Augustine (354–430), a defender of just war, insisted that even when waging war the intention of a Christian should be, strictly speaking, not to kill the enemy but to prevent the enemy from doing great evil (see chap. 18).

We can sum up the two Christian convictions discussed so far as follows:

1. Our biological lives are not our highest good, so death is not the greatest evil.
2. Our biological lives are a precious gift from God, and intentionally terminating our lives is an evil.

Together, these two convictions should guide Christian reflection on political questions concerning end-of-life issues.

These issues involve two related but distinct matters: death itself and the experience of dying. Let's first take up the second, often discussed under the rubric of "the good death," though we in fact experience only dying, not death itself, as either good or bad. A good death depends in part on the circumstances of life, on life going well for people even as they are dying. Christians ought to promote cultures and social arrangements in which a good death is the norm. In particular, we should advocate for affordable and medically responsible hospice care.

- We should resist tendencies in the medical world to consider hospice a cowardly surrender of the fight against death. And we should make hospice accessible to all, especially the poor.
- In addition to alleviating the physical discomforts of the dying, we should care for their psychological, social, and religious needs. Loneliness, for instance, is among the great scourges of old age in modern societies; we should make sure that no one has to die alone (see chap. 13). Similarly, facing our final hour, we are gripped by questions of ultimate concern: we reflect on the character and value of our lives, we may be troubled about relationships that are broken, and we may worry about what is to come. We should make sure that no one has to die without the help of a minister, priest, rabbi, or imam should she want it (see chap. 20).

Dying well isn't, of course, just a matter of getting the right social services. It depends also on leading our lives well through their entire course and doing so even at their very end—on being able to surrender, to reconcile with those we have wronged and those who have wronged us, on the hope of a new beginning in our ending. Such readiness to die can then become "the first step of the resurrection into divine life."[5]

The end-of-life questions that concern death itself rather than the experience of dying are becoming more and more pressing in societies with increasing biotechnological capabilities and expanding elderly populations (in the United States, to name just one advanced industrialized country, the percentage of the population over sixty-five tripled between 1910 and 2010).[6] To address these questions well, let's first clear the ground by distinguishing some terms.

Euthanasia is the intentional killing of a human being for the sake of sparing him from severe suffering.[7] Euthanasia can be self-inflicted (suicide) or performed by another person. It can be *voluntary* (if the person deliberately requests or agrees to be killed), *nonvoluntary* (if the person is unable to consent), or *involuntary* (if the person is unwilling to consent or is not consulted at all). The most commonly debated form of euthanasia today is *physician-assisted suicide*, or PAS for short. PAS refers to any voluntary euthanasia in which a medical doctor provides or helps administer a lethal drug.[8] The core questions that PAS and euthanasia more broadly raise are: (1) Is it ever morally acceptable to actively hasten death's arrival? (2) If so, under what conditions is it acceptable? (3) Regardless of our moral judgment about the matter, should some forms of euthanasia be legal?

Distinct from euthanasia and PAS is the *removal or withholding of life-preserving treatment*. Often, medical treatment can keep alive a person who would otherwise die (or at least keep him in a befuddling ambiguous state with some of the hallmarks of life but not others). This might be as simple as suturing a wound that would otherwise cause massive blood loss or as complicated as making up for failing lung and kidney functions with a ventilator and dialysis. Removal or withholding of life-preserving treatment is just what it sounds like: taking away care that is sustaining life or declining to give treatment that would sustain life. As the medical treatment required increases in complexity and cost and the liveliness of the person decreases, questions arise about whether it is morally acceptable to remove or withhold treatment and who is competent to make that decision and under what circumstances. If euthanasia and PAS raise the question of whether it can be acceptable to hasten death's arrival, withdrawal of treatment brings up the issue of when it is appropriate or legitimate to stop trying to hold death at bay.

Christian ethicist Gilbert Meilaender neatly summarizes the principle that should govern our stance toward these questions: "Though we might properly cease to oppose death while aiming at other choiceworthy goods in life . . . we ought never aim at death as either our end or our means."[9] Since none of us are our own but rather are God's, and since all of us are precious to God, we ought not to intentionally bring about the death of any human being, including ourselves.[10] Euthanasia and PAS are morally wrong. No human being has the right to intentionally take human life: we have self-determination within life, not about its continuation. At the same time, though life is a precious gift, death is not the greatest evil. Clinging to life as if it were a "second God" idolizes life and makes death out to be worse than it is.[11] In sum, we should neither refuse to acknowledge death when it comes nor hasten ourselves or a fellow human being toward death.[12]

Summing up our argument so far we can say:

- Human life is not the highest good. We can and sometimes ought to sacrifice our life for the greater good, and we should not seek to prolong life at any cost.
- Human life is absolutely inviolable. No one has the right to violate my integrity, let alone take life from me; I myself have no right to give up being a bearer of rights (say, by enslaving myself), and I have no right to take my own life.

Christians should insist that terminally ill patients and their agents have the right to waive treatment[13] and should oppose legalization of euthanasia and PAS. The first point is not especially controversial. The second is, so an explanation is in order. We argued above that PAS is morally wrong, but not everything that's morally objectionable should be illegal. So, why prohibit PAS? It is important to distinguish between public policies that merely allow people to do something morally wrong and those that are apt to create a culture in which people are *pressured* to do something wrong. Legalized PAS is likely to fall into the latter category, and our opposition to its legalization is based on this likelihood. A society in which PAS is legal would likely become one in which PAS is expected. Those diagnosed with terminal medical conditions would be seen as selfishly burdening others (the medical system and their families, in particular) if they didn't request PAS.

For millennia, doctors have pledged not to take lives as part of their practice. Once PAS is legalized in some cases, the possibility opens for administering death as medical treatment. If it is permissible for doctors to kill terminally ill patients who wish to die, what about those with nonterminal chronic pain? And the severely disabled? Those who are simply tired of life? Arguments for PAS are based on the right to self-determination, a purported right to exit from life. Once you accept that right, there are no grounds to deny a request for euthanasia for loneliness, for instance, a point Wim Distelmans, a doctor and prominent advocate of Belgium's liberal euthanasia legislation, explicitly makes.[14]

Room for Debate

There is an endless stream of debatable questions about end-of-life issues, a subject in which hard cases are easy to come by and technological changes are always offering new possibilities and new challenges. To name two particularly important ones:

- *Who ought to be able to make end-of-life decisions?* For a patient who has not designated someone with power of attorney or specified in a living will the degree of extreme measures to be taken to preserve her life, on whom should the power and burden of the decision fall? Under what conditions should physicians assume the responsibility of making these decisions?

- *Is there a point at which patients or their agents should no longer have the right to demand treatment? If so, how do we determine where it is?* This is less clear-cut than the right to refuse treatment. Is it wrong to force someone to acknowledge the imminent arrival of death? Should people be permitted to spend themselves into bankruptcy to keep loved ones minimally alive? At what point should insurances refuse to fund postponement of death?

Resources for Further Reflection

Introductory Reading

Cahill, Lisa Sowle. "The Art of Dying." *Sojourners*, June 2010. http://sojo.net/magazine/2010/06/art-dying. Cahill asks how Christians can prepare for a good death as a way of thinking through issues of end-of-life care.

Kaveny, Cathleen. "Dignity and the End of Life: How Not to Talk about Assisted Suicide." *Commonweal*, June 30, 2011. https://www.commonwealmagazine.org/dignity-end-life. Kaveny explains the important differences between abortion and physician-assisted suicide, arguing that the culture-war approach to the former is not adequate to the latter.

Meilaender, Gilbert. "Euthanasia and Christian Vision." *Thought* 57 (1982): 465–75. Through a series of careful distinctions, Meilaender considers the morality of euthanasia "from within the parameters of Christian belief."

US Conference of Catholic Bishops. "To Live Each Day with Dignity: A Statement on Physician-Assisted Suicide." June 16, 2011. http://www.usccb.org/issues-and-action/human-life-and-dignity/assisted-suicide/to-live-each-day/upload/bishops-statement-physician-assisted-suicide-to-live-each-day.pdf. This document is the US bishops' first full statement explaining their opposition to physician-assisted suicide.

Advanced Study

Anscombe, G. E. M. "Murder and the Morality of Euthanasia." In *Human Life, Action, and Ethics: Essays by G. E .M. Anscombe*, edited by Mary Geach and Luke Gormally, 261–78. Charlottesville, VA: Imprint Academic, 2005. With characteristic rigor and intelligence, Anscombe discusses the question of murder in cases of euthanasia and omission of care.

Gill, Robin, ed. *Euthanasia and the Churches*. London: Cassell, 1998. This useful volume contains essays by theologians and ethicists wrestling with the question of euthanasia. Each essay is followed by four responses, and the main contours of the debate are described in the conclusion.

Hauerwas, Stanley, with Richard Bondi. "Memory, Community, and the Reasons for Living: Reflections on Suicide and Euthanasia." In *The Hauerwas Reader*, edited by John Berkman and Michael Cartwright, 577–95. Durham, NC: Duke University Press, 2001. This essay turns attention from problem cases that presuppose we already know what counts as suicide and euthanasia to the communal and moral background assumptions through which these categories are created.

Ramsey, Paul. "On (Only) Caring for the Dying." In *The Patient as Person: Explorations in Medical Ethics*, 113–63. 2nd ed. New Haven: Yale University Press, 2002. In this classic text of theological bioethics, Ramsey explores "the moral limits properly surrounding efforts to save life" and works through a number of crucial conceptual distinctions that illuminate various cases.

15

MIGRATION

> As God is welcoming and just toward all humans, so our societies ought to be welcoming and just toward migrants. We should care especially for those who have been pushed from their homes by violence or dire poverty.

As the well-publicized plight of African and Middle Eastern migrants crossing the Mediterranean to Europe in 2015 has brought to public attention, more people are on the move across borders and within countries today than ever before. In 2013, 232 million people worldwide had lived for more than a year outside their country of birth. Over 740 million have migrated within their home countries. In 2014, nearly 60 million lived as refugees. Every year war, poverty, and natural disaster displace millions from their homes. Many seek a new life—safer, less impoverished, more promising—in a new place.[1]

Jesus was a migrant. When he was a child, his family fled Judea for Egypt as refugees from a government campaign of mass murder (Matt. 2:13–18). Later in life, as a Judean-born Galilean, Jesus wandered between Galilee, Syria, Samaria, and Judea. What would faithfulness to this migrant messiah look like in today's world of massive migrations of people across much firmer borders than those in place when Mary and Joseph took Jesus to Egypt? Whatever else it might entail, surely it will involve welcoming those who are far from home.[2] Jesus himself says, explaining the entrance of the righteous into the eschatological kingdom, "I was a stranger and you welcomed me. . . . Just as you did it to one of the least of these who are members of my family, you did it to me" (Matt. 25:35, 40). Faithfulness to Christ requires welcoming those who find themselves without a home, without resources, without friends in a strange land.

Christians are called not just to welcome Christ the stranger but also to *imitate* Christ the welcomer. Christ is the incarnation of a welcoming God. As creator, God welcomes each of us into God's own world ("the earth is the LORD's" [Ps. 24:1]), offering a place for us and inviting us to work and make a home in it. As the one who makes "all things new" (Rev. 21:5), God welcomes us into the kingdom of heaven. "In my Father's house there are many dwelling places," Jesus says, and he promises to prepare a place for us there (John 14:2). And when we trash the home we've been given and reject the one who gave it, squandering any right we might have claimed to reside with God—when we act like the prodigal son throwing away his inheritance—God welcomes us back with open arms. We all have alienated ourselves from God. We have all made ourselves strangers. And yet God still invites us in. The appropriate response to this divine welcome is to receive it and imitate it.

Note that God's welcoming isn't mere hospitality. We have been given space in God's world, but not as perpetual guests. Instead, we belong; the creation is our homeland, and we are called to make homes for ourselves in it. Ephesians proclaims, "You are no longer strangers and aliens, but are *citizens* with the saints and also *members* of the household of God" (2:19, emphasis added). God makes citizens of aliens and family of strangers. So, too, should we.

When we do for others what God has done for us, we don't just do as God commands and act as God exemplifies. We also become who we are made to be. When encounters with others go well, we become more ourselves. As persons and communities, we are not created to have hermetically sealed identities. Indeed, when we are bent on having such identities, we do violence to ourselves and to others—as in many instances of persons and communities insisting on the "purity" of their soil, blood, or culture. We are at our best when our identities are strong but porous, when our difference is "soft," when we live as "catholic persons," genuinely being ourselves just by welcoming and integrating in our own particular way the wealth of all humanity.[3]

Embracing others is just what love of neighbor looks like when our neighbor is a "stranger." Such welcoming love is the first basic Christian commitment that should shape public engagement related to migration. It's not the only one, though. We must also attend to justice. The countries between which people mostly migrate have histories of mutual relations, often marred by injustice and exploitation. For example, in the 1980s hundreds of thousands of Central Americans fled murderous military regimes and sought refuge in the United States.[4] Because the United States supported these regimes and so was complicit in the violence the refugees fled, it should have acted, as a matter of justice, with the presumption that they ought to receive asylum. Instead, the government refused to recognize them as refugees at all and deported many of them. Decrying this injustice, a number of Christian communities provided sanctuaries for the refugees. Rather than reconsider its policy, the government went so far as to prosecute some of those Christians for "smuggling" migrants. To respond faithfully to migration today, we have to consider what historical injustices have pushed people from their homes and then discern what justice requires of countries that contributed to those injustices.

Political debates about migration issues in destination countries tend to play out merely in terms of economic interests and cultural integrity rather than welcoming embrace and justice. When economic interests and cultural integrity are our main values, the assumption is that things ought to stay as they are; what needs justification, we then believe, is not the rejection of migrants but their reception into a host country. The questions we then ask are: Why should we let strangers in at all? If we do, how many and what kind can we afford to let in? What should we do about undocumented aliens? But if embrace and justice are our main values, the assumption will be that we should welcome *every* stranger in dire need; what needs justification then is not their reception into destination countries but their rejection. The relevant questions are then: Should we put limits on immigration? If we do, what genuine goods do these limits serve?

The primary values that should shape Christian public engagement with migration are embrace and justice. But immigration has to be "managed." There are legitimate limits to immigration, and these are set by two important goods they serve.

1. *Security*. Governments have a prima facie responsibility to protect their citizens. Monitoring and restricting entry to their territory is an indispensable part of exercising that responsibility. But security is a highly subjective good; it depends perhaps more on the intensity of our fears than on the absence of actual threats. We should base our security concerns on facts about immigrants rather than justifying xenophobia and a proclivity to exclusion by appeals to the need for security.

2. *Preservation of a society's ways of life*. The variety of human cultural groups is a genuine good and one that is meant to endure.[5] Every biblical vision of the world to come includes a diversity of nations. Revelation describes the denizens of that world: "a great multitude that no one could count, from every nation, from all tribes and peoples and languages, standing before the throne and before the Lamb, robed in white, with palm branches in their hands" (7:9).[6] All other things being equal, it's a good thing for distinct peoples and groups to continue to

exist (though, of course, cultures are neither "pure" nor static but always changing in encounter with other cultures as well as economic, political, technological, and intellectual developments). But groups can continue to exist only if they maintain some boundaries.

In thinking through how pursuit of embrace and justice, along with legitimate concern for security and cultural integrity, relates to the concrete issues of migration today, it's helpful to make some distinctions. There are several different types of issues related to migration as well as different categories of migration.

- *"Pull" migration*: Migration of those in situations of relative stability and comfort driven by the appeal of another country, usually its opportunities for greater economic attainment.

- *"Push" migration*: Migration driven by the threat of violence or extreme poverty. These migrants are "pushed" from their homes to find whatever opportunity they can elsewhere. Among such migrants, there's an important difference between *refugees*, who flee violence, and the *economically desperate*, who flee extreme poverty.

- *Migration crises*: Situations that prompt a large number of people to leave their home countries suddenly or under intense pressure.

- *Immigration policies*: The sets of regulations about which and how many people are permitted to relocate to a country, as well as the procedures for them to do so.

- *Migrant smuggling*: Moving people without documentation across international borders. Smuggling is extremely hazardous for migrants. According to the Missing Migrants Project, more than 5,200 migrants died trying to reach a destination country in 2015, the majority on the arduous Mediterranean passage to Europe.[7] It's also big business. Smuggling between Mexico and the United States alone grossed more than $5 billion annually as of 2003.[8]

If we cross-pollinate the Christian convictions and the distinctions we've just made, three imperatives follow:

- *Host countries should prioritize receiving "pushed" over "pulled" migrants.* From a Christian perspective, immigration should be primarily a matter not of drawing "those who can best contribute" to the host country[9] (say, enhancing a destination country's economic competitiveness by attracting top engineers) but of caring for the needy and doing justice.
- *Refugees should be the top priority in immigration policy.* They have very few prospects of having their needs met in their countries of origin. Only dramatic political change could make that possible. In contrast, the needs of economically desperate migrants could conceivably be met in ways that allow them to stay in their countries of origin (e.g., foreign aid).
- *It's important to address the roots of migration crises while not ignoring the needs of today's migrants.* Proper response to migration crises calls for more than generous and just immigration policies in destination countries; it demands concerted efforts to eradicate root causes of migration in departure countries and international relations (e.g., war and poverty).

Room for Debate

- *Where is the right balance between welcoming the stranger and the goods of cultural integrity and security at a given time and place?* What's fitting for one context isn't necessarily right for another. Practical wisdom and discernment are required.
- *What root causes of mass migration does our society have a particular responsibility to help address?* It's unlikely that

any one society could address all the crises and injustices that push people to migrate, so we ought to deliberate about where to direct our society's energies. Bear in mind, investing them anywhere is better than nowhere.

Resources for Further Reflection

Introductory Reading

Allen, John. "The Politics of Welcoming the Immigrant—Ruth 2:1–23." *Political Theology Today*, August 11, 2014. http://www .politicaltheology.com/blog/the-politics-of-welcoming-the -immigrant-ruth-21-23/. Allen argues that the second chapter of Ruth implies that our relationship to migrants generates ethical obligations. From this, he very schematically suggests some correctives to current immigration language in the US political sphere.

Scaperlanda, Michael. "Tragic Compassion." *First Things*, June 19, 2014. http://www.firstthings.com/web-exclusives/2014/06 /tragic-compassion. Scaperlanda acknowledges the necessity of immigration reform in the United States but argues that "amnesty-first" strategies—some of which are genuine efforts to shape policy around the norm of compassion—have failed and will continue to fail in tragic ways.

Simpson, Timothy F. "The Politics of Immigration: Genesis 12:1– 4a." *Political Theology Today*, March 10, 2014. http://www .politicaltheology.com/blog/the-politics-of-immigration -genesis-121-4a/. Simpson argues that God's command to Abram to leave his family and God's promise to make him the father of many nations inaugurate a "motif" in the Bible of committing to unsettledness. He claims that the text calls us to treat all strangers—including and especially migrants from other countries—as though they are Abram.

Advanced Study

Groody, Daniel G., and Giocacchino Campese, eds. *A Promised Land, a Perilous Journey: Theological Perspectives on Migration.* Notre Dame, IN: University of Notre Dame Press, 2008. The text provides a breadth of theological perspectives on migration (with a focus on Mexico and the United States) and a host of ancillary issues. Donald Kerwin's essay argues that immigrants are owed certain treatments in virtue of their natural rights and that current US policies fail to take those rights-claims seriously.

Heyer, Kristin. *Kinship across Borders: A Christian Ethic of Immigration.* Washington, DC: Georgetown University Press, 2012. Heyer critiques discussions of immigration that focus on security, legality, or economic prosperity and exclude language of justice and solidarity.

Snyder, Susanna. "Encountering Asylum Seekers: An Ethic of Fear or Faith?" *Studies in Christian Ethics* 24 (2011): 350–66. Snyder argues that in the Bible one finds two ethics of immigration: one of fear and one of faith. She suggests that while faith-based organizations in the UK have often assumed the faith stance toward asylum, these organizations must acknowledge and seriously engage public attitudes of fear.

16

POLICING

Policing is indispensable to protect citizens from harm and create conditions for the flourishing of all. Policemen and policewomen are not warriors fighting an enemy but guardians protecting communities with which they should identify. We should task the police with acting above all as protectors of the poor and underprivileged.

After a police officer shot Michael Brown in Ferguson, Missouri, in 2014, policing became the subject of widespread public discussion in the United States. The demonstrations in the aftermath of the shooting prompted the media to give more attention to subsequent police killings of unarmed Black citizens and taught many White Americans what Americans of other groups have known for decades: a good relationship between a community and its police force, essential to good policing, can't be taken for granted. As in many American neighborhoods, so also in many countries, citizens (sometimes rightly) perceive the police as an enemy—insufferably arrogant, arbitrarily violent, and often corrupt. Yet policing is an indispensable social service. Its purpose is to protect a community from harm caused by its own members or individual visitors from abroad and thus contribute to the security vital to both individual flourishing and communal well-being.

Five imperatives should shape Christian engagement with the complex issues surrounding policing:

1. *Seek peace.* In Jeremiah 29, God commands the people of Judah to seek the peace of Babylon, where they are being taken into exile (Jer. 29:7). Like the Judeans, Christians are called to pursue the peace of the places in which we live. Peace here isn't just the absence of violence or a semblance of order enforced by intimidation and overwhelming force. Rather, it is *shalom*, "a continuing state of communal well-being that is wide and deep and sustainable."[1] That's why the NIV translates this verse "seek the *peace and prosperity* of the city," and the NRSV, "seek the *welfare* of the city" (emphasis added). Followers of Christ, the Prince of Peace, must be committed to policing that is limited neither to preventing violence from spreading nor to imposing what Martin Luther King Jr. called the "obnoxious negative peace" that papers over discord and injustice.[2] We should advocate for more: policing that aims at *shalom*.

2. *Defend the poor.* "The LORD is a God of justice" (Isa. 30:18) and therefore commands us to "establish justice in the gate" (Amos 5:15). When we pursue justice, we move with the grain of a world created and loved by the one true and just God.[3] Among the defining features of divine justice and its human echoes is an unyielding insistence on treating the poor rightly (see chap. 8). To seek justice is to counter the tendency of laws, legal judgments, and law enforcement to treat the poor and weak more harshly than the rich and powerful. Isaiah says of the messiah (whom Christians recognize as Jesus Christ), "With righteousness he shall judge the poor, and decide with equity for the meek of the earth" (Isa. 11:4). Correspondingly, Psalm 72:4 prays that the king will "defend the cause of the poor of the people, give deliverance to the needy, and crush the oppressor." Christians must advocate for policing

practices that don't favor the well-off and the powerful or let them "trample on the heads of the poor" (Amos 2:7 NIV).

3. *Don't act out of fear.* Reading the Gospels, you'll find Jesus constantly telling people not to be afraid. There's no other command that Jesus gives more frequently.[4] Perhaps most importantly for the subject of policing, he says to his disciples, "Do not fear those who kill the body but cannot kill the soul; rather fear him who can destroy both soul and body in hell" (Matt. 10:28). Fear often distorts public debates about policing. The wider public fears crime, civil unrest, and terrorism. The White public fears Black men. People living in poor and minority neighborhoods fear the police. And police officers fear for their lives and safety. While it's important to acknowledge these various fears (some of which are more rationally grounded than others), letting them drive our judgments and our actions will only feed mistrust, hostility, and violence. Christians should resist fear-based arguments and policies about policing that exaggerate threats, turn a blind eye to justice, and undermine peace.[5]

4. *Seek the truth—and tell it.* As followers of Christ, who *is* the truth (John 14:6), we must seek the truth. And we must speak it in love (Eph. 4:15), for God is love and calls us to love. In a world marred by sin, we will have to listen to and speak hard truths without flinching. We can't paper over the histories of racism, ethnic or religious prejudice, and injustice that shape the realities of policing today. We can't ignore the powerful implicit biases that shape our actions while hardly leaving a trace on our conscious thoughts.[6] We can't pretend, for instance, that there's no tendency to see Black boys as older than they are and as more responsible for their actions than their non-Black peers, thus leading to harsher treatment of those boys at the hands of police and the legal system.[7]

5. *Love your neighbors.* Good policing requires love of neighbor. At its best, it is a mode of effective care for them. It can interrupt violent or harmful situations and restore security for people who have been endangered or violated. Well-functioning police forces

don't judge guilt and innocence; that is for the courts. The police protect people from harm and restore order to civic community. As always, love of neighbor ought to be universal (Matt. 5:43–45; Luke 10:25–37). Those who make decisions about policing must love *all* their neighbors, regardless of race or class or culture, and recognize that they all are worthy of protection and care. So, too, police themselves must value the lives and well-being of every person they encounter.

The police focus on domestic security. This distinguishes them from the military, which focuses on national security. The difference is decisive, and it is particularly pronounced in democracies, whose governments are of the people, by the people, and for the people, to use Lincoln's history-making phrase. At the most fundamental level, police and citizens aren't two opposing groups; the police are the people protecting themselves.[8] As soon as a police force starts to see itself as akin to an occupying force in the midst of a hostile, suspect population, it loses touch with the purpose that justifies it.

We entrust the police with an extraordinarily difficult, in some ways even impossible, task. Every time they intervene, there is the possibility that they have misread the situation (it was not a gun but a toy), that they will use excessive force (a restraining maneuver becomes a life-threatening chokehold), or that their intervention will escalate the situation (a confrontational intervention triggers riots rather than restoring peace). The distinguishing feature of the police, compared to other government institutions concerned with domestic affairs, is that they are given the right to use the state's coercive power to enforce the law. That puts them—much more frequently than most other people, including government officials—in situations in which it might be necessary to use potentially lethal force. Lethal force is legitimate only when used in direct defense of the lives of the innocent. But it is difficult to discern accurately and often in a split second when there is actually a threat to innocent lives. Making that determination is an extraordinary responsibility. Even to succeed at this task, to kill only when there is no better way, is tragic; to fail at it, to kill when one should not, is catastrophic.

As the police protect the innocent from harm, they might have to risk their own lives; a tragic number of them are in fact killed on duty. Fifty-one law enforcement officers were killed on duty during "felonious incidents" in 2014 in the United States, making police officers the second-most likely occupation to be victims of homicide on the job, after taxi drivers and chauffeurs.[9] But the more police seek to eliminate risk to their own lives, the more likely they are to err on the side of force and thus risk taking others' lives unjustifiably, sometimes even harming the innocent in the name of protecting the innocent. In 2015, the first year for which relatively comprehensive data are available, police officers in the United States killed 1,136 people, a strikingly disproportionate number of them Black men.[10] In fact, a Black man 18 to 34 years old was more likely to be killed by a police officer in 2015 (3.19 instances per 100,000) than a White American adult was to be killed by *anybody at all* in 2014 (2.52 per 100,000).[11]

Part of the difficulty of policing is that the coercive power we grant the police is subject to profound distortions. The police aren't always right. The *laws* aren't even always right. This may be obvious, but it's important to emphasize for those who tend to turn a blind eye to police abuses. The possible varieties of distortion here are many (just as there are many ways for the police to protect the community rightly).

- Straightforward corruption still devastates public trust in the police in many countries around the world, including communities like Ferguson in the United States.[12]
- In many places, especially cities, the police take an adversarial stance toward the citizens they are supposed to protect, seeing themselves as warriors in enemy territory rather than guardians of citizens' lives.[13]

- Racial biases both implicit and explicit are a constant threat to the integrity of the police force's use of coercion.

The preceding discussion of the police's mission, the potential distortions of that mission, and the five imperatives that ought to frame Christian perspective on policing lead us to highlight five goals toward which we should aim.

- *Police officers ought to be guardians of citizens' lives, not warriors.* Except perhaps in extreme situations like Mexico's drug empires, the police are not trying to reconquer territory or defend it from an "enemy's" attack. They are protecting a community from the potential harm that its own members might cause it. Police weaponry should match this purpose and not imitate the military.

- *Police should be trained in skills for protecting the community without using coercion.* This is particularly important if a society is relying on the police to respond to such social issues as mental illness and homelessness. (Whether it is wise to task police with responding to these issues is an important question in its own right.)

- *The law must avoid putting the police in a position of opposition to the community's population.* Too many municipal codes and policies in the United States effectively criminalize the whole population—for instance, by relying on fines from minor infractions to fund local government and then penalizing poor citizens with escalating harshness when they can't pay them. Such legal structures make nearly anyone an "offender" to the police and the police a threat to the livelihood of everyone who is poor.

- *Public policy and police department cultures should provide needed support for officers without giving blanket protection to officers who break the law or violate proper procedures.* It is important that officers trust that their livelihood and even freedom aren't in jeopardy when they make any misjudgment at all. But it is at least as important that officers who commit serious wrongdoings are judged accordingly and that communities be protected from further harm at their hands.

- *An independent office should be responsible for judging when officers have used force illicitly.*

Room for Debate

- *What weapons should the police routinely carry?* Could certain officers in certain places perform their duties without a firearm? What nonlethal options are available and would be best?

- *What forms of surveillance of police officers will help reduce abusive uses of force?* How much video should be required to be taken of police actions? How should it be shared?

Resources for Further Reflection

Introductory Reading

Coates, Ta-Nehisi. "The Myth of Police Reform." *Atlantic*, April 15, 2015. http://www.theatlantic.com/politics/archive/2015/04 /the-myth-of-police-reform/390057/. Debates about police reform, Coates argues, are too narrow; we need a larger conversation about how many of our social problems we try to solve with violence.

Friedersdorf, Conor. "Ferguson's Conspiracy against Black Citizens." *Atlantic*, March 5, 2015. http://www.theatlantic.com /national/archive/2015/03/ferguson-as-a-criminal-conspiracy -against-its-black-residents-michael-brown-department-of -justice-report/386887/. This article highlights stories and statistics from the Department of Justice's report on Ferguson; the stunning abuses, particularly against African Americans, raise pressing questions about contemporary policing.

Jennings, Willie James. "After Ferguson: America Must Abandon 'Sick Christianity' at Ease with Violence." *Religion Dispatches*, December 9, 2014. http://religiondispatches.org/after-ferguson -america-must-abandon-the-sick-christianity-at-ease-with-vio lence/. The moment of Ferguson, Jennings argues, is about the violence with which Christians have become too comfortable in the name of "law and order."

Winright, Tobias. "Statement: Catholic Theologians for Police Reform and Racial Justice." *Catholic Moral Theology*, December 8, 2014. http://catholicmoraltheology.com/statement -of-catholic-theologians-on-racial-justice/. Signed by over four hundred Catholic theologians and ethicists, this statement calls for reform in policing, especially in regard to racial injustice.

Advanced Study

Balko, Radley. *Rise of the Warrior Cop: The Militarization of America's Police Forces*. New York: PublicAffairs, 2013. This fascinating history of policing in the United States tells the story of increasing militarization and ends with suggestions for how to correct this trend.

Friesen, Duane K., and Gerald W. Schlabach, eds. *At Peace and Unafraid: Public Order, Security, and the Wisdom of the Cross*. Scottdale, PA: Herald, 2005. This collection of essays emerged from a two-year project in which scholars from churches committed to pacifism engaged with theological questions of public order and security.

Taylor, Mark Lewis. *The Executed God: The Way of the Cross in Lockdown America*. Minneapolis: Augsburg Fortress, 2001. This radical theological critique of "lockdown America" includes treatment of the way policing is implicated in larger problems with the criminal justice system.

17

PUNISHMENT

Because Christ is the end of retribution, punishment should not be a payback for the offense. When we punish offenders, we should do so in ways that protect society from harm, honor the humanity of both victims and offenders, aim to reintegrate offenders into society, and promote the prospect of reconciliation between offenders, victims, and their communities.

The United States has the largest prison population in the world. As of 2013, over 2.2 million people were held in American prisons and approximately 10.2 million in prisons worldwide. Of every 100,000 people in the United States, 716 were prisoners. It's hard to say that American prisons are successfully "reforming" all these inmates. A 2014 study found that 77 percent of former prisoners were arrested for a new crime within five years of release. While imprisoned, inmates are often subject to degrading treatment and sometimes outright abuse. Almost 10 percent of youth in the juvenile detention system report being sexually victimized by another prisoner or staff within the last year. The prison system has a staggeringly disproportionate impact on Black Americans.

While 12 percent of American adults are Black, 40 percent of the prison population is.[1] The situation calls out for careful reflection and faithful engagement.

As a starting point for reflection on crime and punishment, let's consider the story of Jesus and the woman caught in adultery, at the time a capital offense. Jesus's remarkable response to the test the scribes and Pharisees lay before him illuminates the central features of a Christian understanding of punishment and its place in society. Here's the story:

> The scribes and the Pharisees brought a woman who had been caught in adultery; and making her stand before all of them, they said to [Jesus], "Teacher, this woman was caught in the very act of committing adultery. Now in the law Moses commanded us to stone such women. Now what do you say?" They said this to test him, so that they might have some charge to bring against him. Jesus bent down and wrote with his finger on the ground. When they kept on questioning him, he straightened up and said to them, "Let anyone among you who is without sin be the first to throw a stone at her." And once again he bent down and wrote on the ground. When they heard it, they went away, one by one, beginning with the elders; and Jesus was left alone with the woman standing before him. Jesus straightened up and said to her, "Woman, where are they? Has no one condemned you?" She said, "No one, sir." And Jesus said, "Neither do I condemn you. Go your way, and from now on do not sin again." (John 8:3–11)

The first thing to take away from this story is that we all make judgments about crime and punishment as sinners and not as fully righteous. Just like the scribes and the Pharisees gathered around the woman, we are not "without sin"—nobody is. We stand under judgment and cannot legitimately adopt the stance of self-righteous judges determining what is to be done with "those" criminals. Acknowledgment of everyone's blameworthiness should inform all our thinking about punishment.

Second, Jesus does not want the woman to be killed. The scribes and Pharisees ask Jesus about the woman's case in order to test him. But the question is only a test if they suspect that Jesus doesn't want to act in accordance with the letter of the book of Holy Laws. Otherwise, there's an easy answer and there's no test: Stone her, and let's move on. The law will have been followed and justice done. The scribes and Pharisees' suspicion is correct. However much Jesus respects the law, he still doesn't want to see this woman executed. This might seem obvious in cultures where adultery is not even a crime. But Jesus's answer makes a larger point: he does *not* relish the death of a sinner—indeed, as the gospel proclaims, he came to die for sinners' salvation. How much less should we savor the suffering of fellow sinners!

Third, even though Jesus doesn't want the woman executed, he still clearly assumes that she has in fact sinned. His final words to her—"Go your way, and from now on do not sin again"—attest to this. She has committed adultery, and that is sin that deserves punishment. But these same final words suggest that the point of the entire story wasn't just to expose the self-righteousness of those who stood in judgment but also to show the grace of forgiveness to offenders deserving punishment and to move the guilty woman to a new way of life, one separated from her past transgression.

A well-ordered criminal justice system deals with the past of the crime and opens up possibilities of a new future for criminals. Looking back to the offense, the state's legal system should *name wrongdoing* through its judgments. While the state should never usurp God's status as ultimate judge, it is important for its representatives to identify wrongs as wrong to the best of their ability. To paper over or completely ignore grievous misdeeds treats wrongdoing as if it were not wrong and thereby wrongs victims and undermines the moral order necessary for common life. Naming wrongdoing tells the truth about it and displays publicly that society doesn't condone it.

But how should those whose wrongdoing the state has publicly named be punished? The most common answer is retribution. Retribution is the principle of eye for eye and tooth for tooth, or rather some rough equivalent of eye and tooth for eye and tooth. Retribution seeks to exact payment from the offender to balance the scales, to pay the debt. It stands in contrast not just to vengeance, which is inflicting pain without a sense of proper measure, but also to forgiveness—that is, not counting the deed against the offender. And that's the problem with retribution from a Christian perspective. Jesus's forgiving the adulteress is for John's Gospel a metaphor of what God did in Jesus Christ with the sin of the entire world. As the Lamb of God he carried the sin of the entire world (John 1:29)—of every human being who has ever lived or will ever live—on the cross of shame. There is no more debt to pay, no weight pressing down to be balanced. As God in Christ forgave, so should we, in our societies no less than in our personal relationships. We name the wrongdoing but don't let it count against the wrongdoer. Christ is the end of retribution.[2]

But Christ is not the end of all punishment. The sort of punishment that is compatible with forgiveness is, in contrast to retribution, forward-looking. We call it generally "correction," as when we use the term *correctional system* as an alternative to *penal system*. Its goal is to make a better person—and a better world—out of one marred by past wrongdoing.

- *We should punish to protect the community from further harm.* We often have reason to worry that those who have committed one crime might commit another. Punishment ought to be shaped in ways that limit the chances that they will. Certain forms of deterrence also fall into this category. Punishment is then like fines for speeding—not a retribution but a means to turn actual and potential offenders away from further offenses.

- *We should punish in ways that facilitate the reform of offenders.* The very act of finding someone guilty of a crime implies that she is responsible for her actions. Yet often offenders need time and assistance to (re)learn to discern right from wrong as well as to grow (back) into agents capable of acting responsibly. Punishment should provide that time and assistance.
- *We should punish in ways that facilitate reconciliation.* When crimes have specific victims, punishment should facilitate the possibility of reconciliation between those victims and the offender. It would be both wrong and impossible to force reconciliation, but since Christians believe that in Christ the world is reconciled to God, we must promote reconciliation among people. Since all crimes harm the community at one level or another, reconciliation between the community and the offender is always needed.

Criminal justice systems throughout history have overwhelmingly failed to live up to this vision of the purposes and ways of punishment. Often they distort punishment by treating it primarily as a matter of retribution. By sending people to prison, we tell ourselves we are "making them pay" for their crimes. We even put on the mantel of the "righteous" ones and relish the suffering and deaths of wrongdoers. The first implication of a Christian understanding of punishment is that we must seek to root out vindictiveness and obsession with inflicting pain from our cultures and institutions of criminal justice.

Here are some other implications of a Christian understanding of punishment:

- *Abolish the death penalty.* The death penalty is the most egregious form of failing to live up to the Christian view of punishment. In countries with secure prison systems, the death penalty provides little to no added protection for the community. Moreover, it is hard to imagine that the death penalty promotes reform or reconciliation; it rather makes them impossible. Short of appealing to retribution, there are no compelling reasons for the death penalty. Christians should therefore strenuously oppose it. But the death penalty is not just wrong in principle; as actually practiced it is also unjust. It is racially biased and biased against the poor, and we can be almost certain that innocent people are executed.[3]

- *Abolish life without parole.* Though a particular prisoner may need to remain incarcerated for life, sentencing an offender to life without parole either decides in advance that the offender is irreformable or assumes that reformation of the prisoner is irrelevant for his or her incarceration.

- *From legislation through trial to punishment, penal systems must be fair.* Without fairness, wrongdoing will not be named truthfully, and the justice system will pervert justice and fail offenders, victims, and the larger society. Failures of fairness differ among societies. In the United States today, the three gravest failures are (1) the near impunity afforded the very wealthy for all but the most flagrantly violent crimes; (2) the criminalization of poverty, as for example in laws that ban sleeping outdoors; and (3) the pervasive racial biases in legislation (e.g., disproportionate mandatory sentences for crack possession),[4] in law enforcement (e.g., racial profiling and the abhorrent pattern of police shootings of Black men),[5] in juries (e.g., convicting Black defendants at higher rates),[6] and among judges (e.g., longer sentences for the same crime for Black defendants).[7]

- *Prison terms should be based not on a supposed standard of proportionate vengeance but rather on the risk prisoners pose to the community, what is most conducive to reform, and what promotes reconciliation.* Significant empirical research is needed to make such a system possible.

- *Prison systems must be arranged to promote reform rather than recidivism.* In most prison systems dehumanizing treatment abounds. Instead of promoting offenders' repentance and reform, it subverts them and therefore, ultimately, does not protect the community either. Today, imprisonment often *increases* the likelihood that offenders will commit another crime in the future.[8] Prisons ought to adopt programs and policies that give offenders a better chance of reforming.[9]

- *Parole regulations and public policies must make it feasible for offenders to reintegrate successfully into society.* It follows from punishment's goals of reform and fostering reconciliation that criminal offenders shouldn't come to the end of prison terms with little chance of obtaining employment, finding housing, or meeting other basic needs.[10]

- *Prisons should not be owned or run by private companies.* Because private prisons profit from having more inmates, they have an interest in growing the prison population. No industry should be based on such perverse incentives, and every prison system will be perverted if it operates with such incentives.

- *Using fines and fees charged to offenders as a strategy for municipal budgeting is unacceptable.* It should go without saying that funding government operations is not one of the purposes of punishment. And yet, in Ferguson, Missouri, for example, 21 percent of the city's total revenue is made up of court fines alone. Neighboring towns see that number as high as 40 percent.[11] Such strategies harm the poor, encourage officials to harass citizens, and in the end depend on making criminals of the very citizens democratic governments are supposed to represent.

Room for Debate

Within the framework of a nonretributive vision for punishment, Christians should debate questions like the following:

- *What are the viable alternatives to incarceration and when should they be used?* Debate about these proposals will probably turn on the question of how best to balance protecting the community from offenders and promoting offenders' reform and reconciliation when those goals conflict.

- *What structures and policies would make our prison systems more conducive to the reform of offenders and their reconciliation with their communities and victims?* There is need for imaginative alternatives, and since the effectiveness of these proposals would be hard to measure without trying them, debate is needed to make the difficult judgments about which proposals are worth exploring.

- *What are the best ways to reduce the prison population?* Sentencing rules (three strikes laws, mandatory minimum sentences, etc.), along with a wide variety of social policies and other factors, influence the rates of crime and incarceration. What mix of approaches will keep more people out of prison and not keep people there longer than necessary?

Resources for Further Reflection

Introductory Reading

Bottum, Joseph. "Christians and the Death Penalty." *First Things*, August 2005. http://www.firstthings.com/article/2005/08/001 -christians-and-the-death-penalty. Bottum argues that Christian revelation should teach us not to idolize the state by allowing it to pursue "blood debt" in executing murderers.

Dulles, Avery Cardinal. "Catholicism and Capital Punishment." *First Things*, April 2001. http://www.firstthings.com/article /2001/04/catholicism-amp-capital-punishment. In this careful and nuanced article, Cardinal Dulles wrestles with the many ambiguities around capital punishment and concludes that on balance Christians should not support it in modern society.

Prunés, Lani. "Mass Incarceration: The Politics behind the Bars." *Sojourners*, June 2015. http://sojo.net/magazine/2015/06/mass-incarceration-politics-behind-bars. This single infographic displays many of the problems with the American criminal justice system.

Stillman, Sarah. "Get Out of Jail, Inc." *New Yorker*, June 23, 2014. http://www.newyorker.com/magazine/2014/06/23/get-out-of-jail-inc. This chilling article documents some of the abuses surrounding the use of fines and the increasing privatization of many aspects of the criminal justice system.

Advanced Study

Alexander, Michelle. *The New Jim Crow: Mass Incarceration in an Age of Colorblindness*. New York: New Press, 2010. In this powerful and well-researched book, Alexander argues that the criminal justice system today functions in much the same way as the Jim Crow laws functioned half a century ago.

Hauerwas, Stanley. "Punishing Christians." In *Performing the Faith: Bonhoeffer and the Practice of Nonviolence*, 185–200. Grand Rapids: Brazos, 2004. What Christians have to offer penal reform, according to Hauerwas, is not a theory of punishment but the witness of a community that punishes for the sake of forgiveness and reconciliation.

Logan, James Samuel. *Good Punishment? Christian Moral Practice and U.S. Imprisonment*. Grand Rapids: Eerdmans, 2008. Logan draws on Hauerwas's account of Christian punishment for the sake of evaluating and seeking to transform the American criminal justice system.

O'Donovan, Oliver. "Punishment." In *The Ways of Judgment*, 101–24. Grand Rapids: Eerdmans, 2005. This chapter defends an account of punishment as a judgment enacted on the person, property, or liberty of the condemned.

18

WAR

We should seek peace both within and between nations. War is never—or almost never—justifiable, and every successful justification has the heavy burden of showing how a particular war is an instance of loving one's neighbors and loving one's enemies.

An estimated 231 million people died in the wars and conflicts of the twentieth century.[1] The early twenty-first century has actually seen a decline in the deadliness of wars, but warfare is hardly a thing of the past. Indeed, for many countries it is an almost ever-present reality. The US military engaged in combat twenty-eight out of the thirty years between 1986 and 2015. British forces fought somewhere in the world every year between 1914 and 2014.[2] Around the world in early 2016, there were still dozens of armed conflicts, some raging, as in Syria, and some simmering but threatening to boil over, as in Kashmir. Worldwide military expenditures in 2014 totaled over $1.7 trillion.[3] War and the pursuit of peace remain pressing issues for public engagement.

Christians are fighting in and supporting many of these ongoing wars. That's not at all unusual. From the French and English knights of the Hundred Years' War to Russian and Ukrainian nationalists in the 2010s, Christians throughout history have displayed a distressing tendency to put their countries before their faith. American Christians have by and large supported every war their country has ever fought, at least at the start. We have assumed that our wars are righteous and neglected our responsibility to critically assess every call to arms.

God is "the God of peace" (Rom. 15:33; Heb. 13:20).[4] That is true, first of all, of God's very being. As Trinity, God is the harmonious interrelation of the three "persons." There is no hostility, no conflict at all, between Father, Son, and Spirit. Because the God of peace created it, the world is meant to be a world of peace. As theologian and ethicist Oliver O'Donovan argues, peace is both the basic *truth* of creation, the world's deepest reality notwithstanding the pervasiveness of violence, and the *goal* of history, that for which, just because of the pervasiveness of violence, everything yearns.[5]

Faithfulness to the God of peace in a world with many theaters of war requires that we "seek peace, and pursue it" (Ps. 34:14b). We cannot accept that war is just the way things are. All Christians must be "pacifists," at least in the sense of being seekers and makers of peace.[6] As Jesus puts it in one of the Beatitudes, "Blessed are the peacemakers, for they will be called children of God" (Matt. 5:9). A principled commitment to peacemaking ought to inform all Christian reflection on conflict of any type, from interpersonal quarrels to international wars.

What does it mean to pursue peace in faithfulness to the God of peace? Most importantly, peace is not just for friends—fellow citizens, coreligionists, those from our civilizational sphere— whereas war is for foes. Christ came as the universal Prince of Peace (Isa. 9:6; Luke 2:14), and therefore Christians must "pursue peace with *everyone*" (Heb. 12:14, emphasis added). Jesus famously radicalized the command from Leviticus to love our neighbor (19:18). In the Sermon on the Mount he says, "You have heard that it was said, 'You shall love your neighbor and hate your enemy.' But I say to you, Love your enemies and pray for those who persecute you, so that you may be children of your Father in heaven, for he makes his sun rise on the evil and on the good, and sends rain on the righteous and on the unrighteous" (Matt. 5:43–45). The commandment to love one's neighbors is a commandment to love *everyone* without exception, enemies no less than fellow citizens.

Since there are no exceptions to the love commandment, support for a war could be justified on Christian grounds only if it could be shown to be a form of love, and love not just for our attacked neighbors but also for the attacking enemies. Thomas Aquinas (1225–74), a key source for what is commonly known as "just-war theory," acknowledges that love is the standard even for decisions about war; he places his consideration of the possible justice of war within his discussion of the virtue of love.[7] In discussions about war and love, it goes without saying that love is not necessarily about warm feelings at all but rather concerns active benevolence and beneficence. Since we must love our enemies, we are justified in waging only wars that aren't simply for our own benefit but are also for the benefit of our enemies.

Building on the work of Aquinas, as well as Augustine before him, Christian thinkers have developed nuanced criteria to guide judgments about the injustice and justice of wars. As a rule, they distinguish between criteria governing when it is just to go to war (*ius ad bellum*) and those governing the just conduct of war (*ius in bello*). The most commonly identified *ius ad bellum* norms are the following:[8]

- *Legitimate authority.* War is to be waged not by private individuals or groups but only by legitimate governing authorities.
- *Just cause.* War is to be waged only in the defense of an innocent population suffering unjust attack. Strictly speaking,

self-defense is not a legitimate cause for war, though defense of an innocent population counts as a reason.

- *Right intention*. A just war must aim at just peace, not at merely squelching the enemy with superior power.
- *Last resort*. War may be undertaken only after all other acceptable means of addressing the injustice are exhausted.
- *Reasonable chance of success*. A just war seeks to address an injustice that it stands a reasonable chance of actually addressing.

The just conduct of war usually includes the following two rules:

- *Discrimination*. Just warriors actively strive to avoid the deaths of noncombatants. That means not only that they will not intentionally carpet bomb population centers but also that they will attack only military targets, refrain from using inherently indiscriminate weaponry like landmines and biological weapons, avoid tactics likely to bring civilians into harm's way, and place their military installations as far from civilians as possible.
- *Proportionality*. The expected cost of a particular tactic or a broader strategy must advance the circumscribed ends of a just war. The costs here are measured not merely in monetary terms but also in destruction of the natural environment, life-sustaining infrastructure, and valuable cultural artifacts, and, above all, in the suffering and deaths of specific human beings, created and loved by God—people for whose salvation Jesus died.

We should interpret all these norms in light of the commandment to love our enemies. If an act can't be loving, it can't be justified on Christian terms. For instance, loving your neighbor is incompatible with intending to kill her. Consequently, a justifiable act of war must be undertaken without the intent to kill. The killing of an enemy ought to be only the lamentable outcome of an unsuccessful attempt to incapacitate her so that she ceases to commit unjust aggression. As Augustine said, "It ought to be necessity, and not your will, that destroys an enemy who is fighting you."[9] Indeed, every time an "enemy" is killed, we ought to bewail that we weren't able to find nonlethal means of stopping his aggression. If this stance sounds unrealistic, even ridiculous, that shouldn't come as a surprise. The demand that a justifiable war be an expression of love of our enemies sets the bar *incredibly* high. This is part of the reason why some Christians think that war can in fact never be justified on Christian grounds.[10]

Loving our enemies will, no doubt, make it harder to win a war against them. It might even be the difference between victory and defeat. More, it is possible that loving our enemies might lead us to refuse to fight against them and to oppose, for instance, armed resistance to invasion. Christian faith requires that we be willing to pay that cost. As Daniel M. Bell Jr. puts it, "Just warriors will suffer defeat or surrender before they will fight unjustly, which means that the just war tradition as a form of Christian discipleship may come to resemble the sacrifice and suffering that is nothing less than a taking up of the cross."[11] To fight unjustly would be to try to achieve good by doing evil.

We've already mentioned some radical and perhaps unsettling implications of a Christian stance toward peace and war. In conclusion, we suggest several more that seem relevant to our particular context.

- *Preventive and preemptive wars in general fail to demonstrate just cause or to be undertaken as last resorts.* There is no guarantee that prospective enemies will in fact attack until they have in fact attacked. The chance always remains that the enemies' intentions have been misinterpreted or that they will reconsider their planned aggression. It is just and loving to give them as much opportunity as possible to do so, rather than to pull the trigger in self-protection first. The implication is not that we shouldn't use coercive means to arrest people plotting a terror attack. For one thing, war isn't the right paradigm for thinking about a case of this sort (the "war on terror" is more like the "war on poverty" than like a literal war). For another, in the case of preventive war, the force that is applied before the supposed enemy has actually attacked is lethal, whereas arrests should at least strive to be minimally forceful.

- *Third-party interventions to interrupt mass killings or protect a people from invasion are less suspect than military actions justified by appeals to "national interest."* National interest is apt to distort our view of justice, lead us into conflicts that do not serve peace, and cause us to fail to love our neighbors, let alone our enemies. Humanitarian interventions at least present a plausible case for being motivated by love of our suffering neighbors and aiming to protect them. That said, we must be wary of using humanitarianism as a moral fig leaf for baser motives.

- *Christians who believe in the possibility of just wars should advocate for policies allowing selective conscientious objection.* Military discipline usually requires that subordinates follow their superiors' orders regardless of the cause a war is being fought for and regardless of the action being taken (with the exception of recognized war crimes). Allowing soldiers to conscientiously object to particular campaigns or refuse particular orders that they are convinced are unjust might in fact be a highly costly, deeply impractical policy. But practicality is not what's at issue here. By refusing to recognize soldiers as moral agents in their own rights, armies treat them as functionally similar to inanimate tools like drones or cruise missiles.

Room for Debate

There is a venerable history of debate about whether Christians can ever justifiably support or wage war. At its best, that debate focuses on the following question: *Could any realistically imaginable war be a form of love of neighbor and enemy in both its cause and its prosecution?* This is the decisive question in the debate between Christian pacifists and just warriors. If the answer is no, then Christians are bound to oppose all wars, with the unsettling consequence that we will have to either advocate refraining to resist with force even the worst aggressors or argue, as Miroslav has in *Exclusion and Embrace*, that when permitting the slaughter of innocents is the only alternative, we should commit acts of violence that are not justifiable on Christian grounds.

Christians convinced that it is possible to give a Christian justification of war would need to find compelling answers to at least the following two questions:

- *What conditions are more likely than others to justify going to war?* In the end, we must make judgments about specific cases on the basis of their particularities, but it is a helpful exercise to debate, for instance, the following questions: Can we justly resist a tyrannical government with force, and if so, who can offer such resistance and under what conditions? What would make military intervention in order to interrupt mass killings justifiable, and in what cases would our prayers, laments, and nonmilitary interventions have to suffice?

- *What modes of engaging in warfare are unjustifiable?* Modern warfare offers an endless stream of new weapons and tactics that anyone who believes in the possibility of just war must assess. Can drone strikes, for instance, be proportionate and sufficiently discriminating? Can they meet the requirement of intention to incapacitate rather than kill?

Once we find ourselves, as we do with distressing frequency, in countries at war, Christians should ask the following:

- *How can we best love our neighbors, both friends and enemies, in the midst of war?* Should Christians support the war effort economically or not? Should we protest? How can we call unjust wars unjust without dishonoring veterans and the families of soldiers killed in combat?
- *What policies are most conducive to justice and love at this specific point in this particular war?* Given that war has begun, what steps can be taken to maximize the justice and lovingness of the way it is carried out?

Resources for Further Reflection

Introductory Reading

Albright, Madeleine, with Bill Woodward. "The Question of Conscience." In *The Mighty and the Almighty: Reflections on America, God, and World Affairs*, 47–64. San Francisco: Harper-Collins, 2006. Albright, a former US Secretary of State, reflects on the immense complexity of reasoning about war and peace as a policymaker. She maintains the possibility of just war and considers the NATO campaign in Kosovo as a possible example.

Bell, Daniel M., Jr. "Just War as Christian Discipleship." Pamphlet 14 in the Renewing Radical Discipleship series, Ekklesia Pamphlets, edited by Daniel M. Bell Jr. and Joel Shuman. Eugene, OR: Wipf & Stock, 2005. http://www.ekklesiaproject.org/wp-content/uploads/2011/05/Ekklesia-14.pdf. Bell challenges Christians to envision the type of disciples we would have to be to become truly just warriors. See also his book by the same title (Grand Rapids: Brazos, 2009).

Hauerwas, Stanley. "Why War Is a Moral Necessity for America." *ABC Religion and Ethics*, October 29, 2010. http://www.abc

.net.au/religion/articles/2010/10/28/3050927.htm. Through a discussion of the Civil War, Hauerwas argues that part of the difficulty of the just-war tradition in America is the ritual function of the sacrifices of war in American politics.

Johnson, James Turner. "Just War, as It Was and Is." *First Things*, January 2005. http://www.firstthings.com/article/2005/01/just-waras-it-was-and-is. Johnson provides an insightful exploration of changes in the just-war tradition in order to call Christians back to its true vision.

Advanced Study

Anscombe, G. E. M. "The Justice of the Present War Examined." In *Ethics, Religion, and Politics: Collected Philosophical Papers*, 72–81. Vol. 3. Minneapolis: University of Minnesota Press, 1981. This criticism of British involvement in World War II, published in England in 1939, gives an excellent example of the rigor required by those committed to the just-war tradition.

O'Donovan, Oliver. *The Just War Revisited*. Cambridge: Cambridge University Press, 2003. O'Donovan defends the just-war tradition by arguing that it is not a method for validating wars nor a set of rules for war but a history of reflection on those situations in which political judgment must be made beyond the scope of its ordinary domestic authority.

Stassen, Glen. *Just Peacemaking: Transforming Initiatives for Justice and Peace*. Louisville: Westminster John Knox, 1992. Stassen aims to present an alternative to the two traditional Christian options of just war and pacifism by turning focus from the justifiability of war to the activity of peacemaking.

Yoder, John Howard. *When War Is Unjust: Being Honest in Just-War Thinking*. Eugene, OR: Wipf & Stock, 1996. The great pacifist theologian John Howard Yoder brings a rigorous analytical mind to the just-war tradition, questioning and probing its various features and raising the possibility that it may no longer be viable.

19

TORTURE

We should never condone torture. Torture dehumanizes both the victim and the torturer; it violates the dignity of the one and degrades the integrity of the other, and it erodes the moral character of the society that permits it.

We can define torture as the intentional infliction of significant and usually repeated physical or psychological harm on people with the aim of breaking down their human integrity and their ability to resist the torturers' will.[1] Officials of the Austrian monarchy in the seventeenth century subjected Protestant Anabaptists to the rack so that they might recant their "heresies" of pacifism and believer's baptism. That was torture. The dictatorship of Augusto Pinochet in Chile burned, shocked, and beat its supposed enemies until they confessed to nonexistent crimes. That was torture. American agents repeatedly waterboarded detainees in the "war on terror," deprived them of sleep, stripped them naked, subjected them to continual deafening noises, confined them to coffin-sized boxes, and beat them in order to "extract" information about terrorist organizations. That too was torture. As this last example suggests, torture is not a thing of the past. From Azerbaijan to Zimbabwe and from the so-called Islamic State to the Zetas drug cartel, states and nonstate actors continue to use torture with alarming frequency.[2] It remains important for Christians to understand how faith should shape their stance toward torture.

As we discuss in chapters 11, 13, 14, and 24, God loves human beings with a radical, value-bestowing love. Out of love, God has also given human beings certain capacities—differing for different people, with no one capacity or set of capacities normative or definitive for humanity as such—among which are in most cases powers to be agents in the world, make judgments, have purposes, and act on those purposes. To intentionally inflict severe pain on such a beloved creature of God is to assault the God who loves her and to mock the value that God's love bestows. To do so with the goal of demonstrating that she is worthless and taking away whatever powers of agency she might have is simply to heap sin upon sin.

Torture, we have said above, dehumanizes its victims. But in an important sense that is not quite right. Nothing any human can do—no crime one can commit, no harm one can suffer—can actually take away the gift of humanity that God has bestowed on each person. Strictly speaking, nothing can dehumanize. And yet there is something to the charge that torture dehumanizes. In torture, the torturers act on the victim as though she weren't a human, as though she were a worthless piece of garbage, a malformed tool in need of being twisted and bent into shape for the torturers' use. When torture "works," it deletes the marks of humanity from a person—victims become without "form or majesty," "despised" creatures from whom all "hide their faces," as it says of the Suffering Servant in Isaiah 53, a passage early Christians applied to the crucified Jesus Christ. Torture also renders the victim less able, or completely unable, to act or recognize himself as the human he is. Though torture is unable to dehumanize its victims in the eyes of God—the eyes that give us humanity and that alone can take it away—it dehumanizes them in human eyes, first in the eyes of the torturers and then, often, in their own eyes as well.

Those who suffer torture aren't, however, torture's only victims. Torture also harms the torturers. It alienates them from God, the source of our very humanity and all our good, as surely as torturing a child would set the torturer at odds with the child's parents. It also alienates them from themselves. Torture dulls torturers' affections and lets their baser instinct take the upper hand under the guise of serving the common good. It also tears them apart internally. Without splitting yourself in two, how could you be both a torturer and a father or friend or loving neighbor? You can come up with justifications—for example, because you love your children, friends, and neighbors, you must torture—but you can rarely quiet the voice of bad conscience. The damage is most acute closest to the act of torture, but it extends to the entire community that sanctions torture. A country that lets its officials torture splits itself in half morally and is apt to become callous toward human life in general. In treating others as if they were less than human, torturers and those who approve of their action treat themselves as less than human. The more they degrade others, the more degraded they become.

Much of the torture that takes place today occurs during interrogations, which are often a critical aspect of security operations. It is therefore important to distinguish between torture and legitimate practices of interrogation. One might think that coercion makes the difference, torture being coercive whereas interrogation is not. But that's not quite right. Since interrogation is the questioning of *detainees*, it inherently involves some degree of coercion. The questioning isn't voluntary. The detainee isn't free to go. She doesn't have to answer questions, but she can't avoid being asked them. Since at least this sort of coercion is necessarily involved, and since interrogation is in principle legitimate, it can't be the case that any and all uses of coercion in interrogation are torture. To test whether a particular practice is torture, we should ask whether it inflicts significant and repeated harm in such a way as to treat the interrogated as less than human, a mere object of manipulation.[3]

In the past, Christians have both approved of torture and practiced it. For example, the Christian Roman emperor Theodosius I (347–95) commanded that clergy not be tortured but permitted torture of lower-class laypeople, and Pope Innocent IV (1195–1254) approved the use of torture in certain church court proceedings.[4] Many Christians approve of torture now, especially in the struggle against terrorism.[5] Yet in a vision of political society faithful to Christ, there is no room for torture. One of the signature Christian teachings is the command to love enemies, a command that follows closely from the character of God as revealed in Jesus Christ. When we permit torture in our names, we fail to be faithful to the gospel of Jesus Christ in our public lives. It is utterly incongruous for the followers of Christ to assent to and even cheer on the torture of those for whose salvation Christ was tortured and died! Christians are called to resist programs of torture, whether they go by the name of "enhanced interrogation techniques" or by some other bureaucratic euphemism. Doing so will quite possibly be unpopular, but it is right. Those of us who live in countries with recent histories of torture should also advocate for just public acknowledgment of those practices and for the prosecution of leaders who violated national or international laws by designing and ordering the implementation of policies of torture.

It is possible that successful abolition of state-sanctioned torture would make us less safe. But not all possibilities turn into realities. The main argument in favor of torture is that torture is necessary to obtain information essential to preventing terrorist acts and other forms of significant harm to a community. Evidence suggests that the argument is false: torture doesn't help interrogation efforts and might even harm them. The ineffectiveness of torture was one of the chief findings of the US Senate Select Committee on Intelligence's report on the CIA's interrogation programs.[6] If

the evidence is correct, that's good news. But if it's false, that
doesn't undercut the case against torture. If doing what is right
comes with a price, we should pay it. Commitment to do right
even when it is dangerous is a central feature of the Christian way
of life exemplified clearly in the story of Jesus Christ (and taught
by many great moral teachers of the past, such as Socrates and
Immanuel Kant). If the unlikely situation arises in which no other
means except torture would save our societies from significant
harm, we should suffer harm rather than commit wrong. To trade
humanity for security is a bad bargain.

In other chapters, we have distinguished between moral and
legal questions and said that answering the former doesn't au-
tomatically answer the latter. There are things that are legal but
are immoral. Only some of them should we seek to make illegal
(for instance, domestic abuse, which was effectively legal in the
United States until the twentieth century); others we should not
criminalize (for instance, defaming a religion). Might torture be
one of those things that are immoral but should still be legally
permissible? Certainly not. Torture violates basic human rights,
something that ought to be illegal for anyone to do, whether a
private citizen or a government official. Moreover, when democratic
governments torture in the name of their citizens, we citizens
become complicit in the egregious wrongdoing of torture. It is
therefore crucial for citizens not only to consider torture morally
wrong but to work to stop their governments from torturing.

(No) Room for Debate

There is simply no legitimate debate for Christians on whether torture is acceptable. But there is room for debate about what exactly
constitutes torture and how to distinguish torture from acceptable
forms of coercion in interrogation. Some practices are clearly
torture when used on captives or for interrogation purposes—for
instance, rape, dismemberment, and mutilation. Others present

harder questions. Is the infliction of physical pain ever acceptable? If so, under what conditions does it turn into torture? What
methods of instilling confusion in detainees are legitimate—for
example, does waking up a detainee in the middle of the night and
immediately peppering him with questions have a dramatically
different moral status from systematic sleep deprivation? Does
the increasing use of solitary confinement in American prisons
amount to a systematic attempt to break down inmates' humanity
and make them into easily pliable objects? And so on.

Because interrogation methods, while they are actually being
used, are hidden in a shroud of secrecy, most ordinary people
will only ever hear about specific "techniques" after the fact. It is,
nevertheless, important to debate the parameters of what does and
doesn't constitute legitimate interrogation and on what grounds,
so that we can judge well and advocate for informed and morally
responsible legislation about the matter. The key issues in the debate about torture are whether interrogation methods treat human
beings as mere manipulable objects and whether they are part of
a program meant to degrade the humanity of the interrogated.
Any Christians who have a voice in the formation of policies related to interrogation have a particular responsibility to consider
deeply whether proposed methods are torture and, if they are, to
denounce them as strongly as possible and as publicly as necessary.

Resources for Further Reflection

Introductory Reading

The Editors. "The Truth about Torture? A Christian Ethics Sym-
posium." *First Things*, January 6, 2010. http://www.firstthings
.com/blogs/firstthoughts/2010/01/the-truth-about-torture-e2
8094-a-christian-ethics-symposium. Eight Christian ethicists
respond to an article in which Charles Krauthammer defends
the moral necessity of torture.

Gushee, David. "5 Reasons Torture Is Always Wrong: And Why There Should Be No Exceptions." *Christianity Today*, February 1, 2006. http://www.christianitytoday.com/ct/2006/february /23.32.html. A leading evangelical ethicist argues that torture violates human dignity and the demands of justice and that it degrades and dehumanizes the torturer as well as the society that supports it.

Meilaender, Gilbert. "Stem Cells and Torture: What a Society Can and Cannot Afford to Do When Its Survival Is at Stake." *Weekly Standard*, June 8, 2009. http://www.weeklystandard .com/article/17649. Meilaender argues that captured terrorists should not be treated by the same standards as captured soldiers but nonetheless rejects torture as an ongoing practice of a "war against terror."

National Association of Evangelicals. "An Evangelical Declaration against Torture: Protecting Human Rights in an Age of Terror." 2007. http://nae.net/an-evangelical-declaration-against-torture/. This strong statement against the use of torture was adopted by the National Association of Evangelicals.

Waldron, Jeremy. "What Can Christian Teaching Add to the Debate about Torture?" *Theology Today* 63 (2006): 330–43. Waldron, a secular legal theorist and philosopher, argues that public debate on torture needs the voice of the churches.

Advanced Study

Biggar, Nigel. "Individual Rights versus Common Security? Christian Moral Reasoning about Torture." *Studies in Christian Ethics* 27 (2014): 3–20. Biggar challenges the idea that aggressive interrogation is torture but still concludes that it should not be morally or legally accepted.

Gordon, Rebecca. *Mainstreaming Torture: Ethical Approaches in the Post-9/11 United States.* Oxford: Oxford University Press, 2014. In contrast to standard accounts of the ethics of torture, which treat it as an isolated act, Gordon conceives of torture as a social practice and evaluates it on these grounds.

Hunsinger, George, ed. *Torture Is a Moral Issue: Christians, Jews, Muslims, and People of Conscience Speak Out*. Grand Rapids: Eerdmans, 2008. Christian, Jewish, and Muslim leaders all speak out against the justifiability of torture. Part 2 of the book provides a compelling Christian defense of an absolute ban on torture.

Porter, Jean. "Torture and the Christian Conscience." *Scottish Journal of Theology* 61, no. 3 (August 2008): 340–58. Taking up Jeremy Waldron's challenge to Christians, Porter argues for an absolute prohibition on the use of torture, primarily on the grounds that it is a direct assault on the image of God.

20

FREEDOM OF RELIGION (AND IRRELIGION)

All people are responsible for the basic direction of their own lives and should be free to shape their lives in accordance with their deep commitments. They should be free to embrace a new faith and abandon the old without suffering discrimination, as well as to bring their own perspectives to bear on public life and to do so on equal terms with everyone else.

Over three-quarters of the world's population live in countries with high levels of government restrictions on freedom of religion. For example, several Indian states have laws against "inducing" or "alluring" someone to convert to another religion. Even in countries that score lower on rankings of government restrictions, religious practice can still be significantly limited. In France, for instance, it is illegal to wear "conspicuous religious symbols" in public schools, and the full-face veil worn by some Muslim women (*niqab*) is prohibited in public places. Worse, in almost a third of countries, people have recently been assaulted or driven from

167

their homes for practicing their religions. Between 2006 and 2009, government or hostile social groups have harassed Muslims in 59 percent and Christians in 66 percent of countries.[1] Freedom of religion cannot be taken for granted, despite the fact that the constitutions of many countries guarantee it.

Restrictions on religious freedom are not a recent phenomenon. Through most of their history, adherents of all world religions have both suffered persecution and persecuted others. Christianity was born and spread for two centuries as a persecuted religion. The religious and political leaders of the time crucified Jesus for blasphemy and sedition. Early Christians were persecuted out of fear of cultural difference and political disloyalty; their contemporaries believed that allegiance to the one God as revealed in Jesus Christ undermined accepted cultural mores and the rule of Caesar. Not long after Christianity became the official religion of the empire, however, Christians themselves started persecuting. For centuries—roughly during periods and in places where the Christian faith and political society were institutionally and ideologically intertwined—Christians insisted on freedom for true believers but denied freedom to those deemed to be heretics and apostates, as well as to adherents of other religions. Leading Christian thinkers advocated various kinds of religious coercion.[2] At the same time, Christians were at the forefront of the struggle for freedom of religion, as the case of Roger Williams (ca. 1603–83) in colonial America amply illustrates.[3]

Before we give reasons why Christians should unequivocally affirm freedom of religion, which we take to include freedom to adhere to no religious faith at all, it is important to recall Scripture's teaching about the persecution of Christians. According to the New Testament, Christians should *expect* to be persecuted. Jesus warns his disciples, "If they persecuted me, they will persecute you" (John 15:20). In the Epistles we read, "All who want to live a godly life in Christ Jesus will be persecuted" (2 Tim. 3:12). Jesus even declares that "those who are persecuted for righteousness' sake" are blessed (Matt. 5:10).

Still, Christians should not seek persecution. Jesus calls us blessed when we suffer abuse *for righteousness' sake* and *on his account*. We are blessed not because we suffer persecution but because Christ and the righteousness of the kingdom of God matter to us more than our comfort. If we aren't persecuted or disadvantaged as Christians, we should examine ourselves to determine whether we have compromised the gospel and failed to follow Christ faithfully. If we are persecuted, we should examine ourselves to determine whether we are being persecuted for Christ and for righteousness. When in the 1970s the IRS denied tax-exempt status to Bob Jones University because it prohibited interracial dating, it was *not* a case of persecution for righteousness' sake!

Since Christians continue to be persecuted widely—according to credible reports, 250 million Christians are suffering persecution today—we have an interest in affirming freedom of religion.[4] But since Christians have a centuries-long track record of persecuting others, can we in fact unequivocally affirm freedom of religion—freedom for all religions, not just our own? We can and we ought to. The freedom to adopt and lead a way of life is the most fundamental human freedom, since our commitment to a way of life shapes every aspect of our existence. This is the freedom that Jesus's own mission presupposed: in response to God's voice at his baptism, Jesus embarked on the mission that led to his death and resurrection. This is also the freedom that Jesus's invitation to his disciples to follow him presupposed: he called Peter and the eleven to a new way of living their Jewish faith.

Reflecting on the nature of human response to God's call, the apostle Paul wrote, "one believes with the heart" (Rom. 10:10). A person becomes a Christian not by mere outward conformity to ambient influences or acquiescence to coercive demands but through embracing a way of life in the very core of one's being. Arguing against the persecution of Christians in ancient Rome, the early church father Tertullian (160–220) articulated the position as a general principle: "It is unjust to compel freemen against their will" to engage in religious rituals, for the gods "can have no desire of offerings from the unwilling."[5]

Together with these early Christians, by far the great majority of Christians today affirm freedom of religion—freedom to embrace, abandon, and live out in private and in public one's own faith. God's call to each of us to align our beliefs and practices with the source and goal of our existence, along with the conviction that this alignment is a matter of heart, presupposes that freedom to respond to God's call in such a way is a positive good. Christians cannot restrict this freedom only to themselves, demanding freedom to be and to live as Christians while denying the freedom of non-Christians to be and to live as non-Christians. It is a failure of nerve to rely on the coercive power of government to foster the Christian faith. God can do just fine without stacking the legal deck in Christianity's favor.[6]

We should work to establish political institutions that embody freedom of religion and equal respect where they are not in place and nurture them where they are. In nations with historically majority-Christian populations, it is tempting for Christians to reject other faiths as "foreign" and restrict their practice. Christians must resist this temptation and stand up for others' right to free exercise of their faith. Christians should support, for instance,

- the right of Muslims to build mosques in the communities in which they live;[7]
- the right of followers of other faiths to use their own sacred texts for public ceremonies like being sworn in for public office and for people of no religious faith to use no sacred text at all;
- the right of Muslims to wear headscarves (and full veils), Jews to wear *kippah*, and Sikhs to wear turbans in all public spaces, no less than Christians to wear crosses;

- the right of ministers who for religious reasons are unable to support the legality of same-sex marriages not to perform such marriage ceremonies and the right of medical professionals who for religious reasons consider abortion unethical not to perform such medical procedures.

In the context of pluralistic democratic societies it is crucial to advocate the right of all people to bring the visions of human flourishing and common good they take from their faiths or philosophies to bear on public life and do so on equal terms with everyone else. Indeed, we should receive their contributions with respect and give them serious critical consideration (which doesn't necessarily mean agreement!).

Room for Debate

- *How should the moral principles of freedom of conscience and equal respect be institutionalized?* In the United States there is a long tradition of the separation of religion and state and—perhaps to a lesser extent—of impartiality of the state toward all overarching interpretation of life, religious and irreligious. These are operative modes designed to make the moral principles of freedom of religion and equal respect possible.[8] Other countries, sometimes no less socially pluralistic than the United States, have institutional arrangements in which religion and state are related much more closely. The form institutions should take is open for debate. The moral principles should not be.

- *How should we decide between competing goods when a religious practice comes into conflict with other public goods?* As is often the case with political questions, the value of freedom of religion will sometimes conflict with other values. In some cases the conflict will result from a poor understanding of either freedom of religion or the other value. For example, it would be a misunderstanding of equal treatment under the law to claim that it required denying a Buddhist prisoner the right to eat vegetarian meals when other prisoners didn't have that choice.[9] But in other cases—such as the decision of a hospital to give a life-saving blood transfusion to the child of Jehovah's Witnesses, whose beliefs forbid the procedure—there will be a genuine trade-off.[10] Since each case will differ, we will have to discern and deliberate each on its own merits.

- *What should qualify for protection under the principles of freedom of religion?* This is a particularly hard instance of the competing-goods question. It asks when it is acceptable to constrain the free exercise of a way of life's central practices. It's hard, maybe impossible, to draw a clear line between which religious practices deserve protection and which can legitimately be outlawed. Certainly some cases are clear—the ability to hold religious services should be protected, for example, while the ability to perform a child sacrifice at those services should not—but many are not. And yet the line has to be drawn. We will always draw this line based on moral commitments—commitments that the people we're proposing to coerce don't share with us. The question therefore demands careful consideration.

Resources for Further Reflection

Introductory Reading

Galston, William A., Michael P. Moreland, Cathleen Kaveny, Douglas Laycock, Mark Silk, and Peter Steinfels. "The Bishops and Religious Liberty." *Commonweal*, May 30, 2012. https://www.commonwealmagazine.org/bishops-religious-liberty. Six Catholic scholars respond to the US bishops' 2012 statement, "Our First, Most Cherished Liberty," which warns against "unprecedented threats" to religious liberty in America.

Garvey, John H. "The Real Reason for Religious Freedom." *First Things*, March 1997. http://www.firstthings.com/article/1997 /03/001-the-real-reason-for-religious-freedom. "Why do we protect freedom of religion?" Garvey asks. The answer, which turns out to be much more complicated than it sounds, is that religion is a good thing.

Volf, Miroslav. "Exclusion or Saturation? Rethinking the Place of Religion in Public." *ABC Religion and Ethics*, March 11, 2014. http://www.abc.net.au/religion/articles/2014/03/11/3960854 .htm. The place of religion in the public sphere, Miroslav argues, should be determined by the center of faith itself; he gives six points describing what this means for Christianity.

———. "Public Engagement." In *A Public Faith: How Followers of Christ Should Serve the Common Good*, 119–37. Grand Rapids: Brazos, 2011. This chapter focuses on the need for respect in political engagement with particular attention to the issue of religious disagreement.

Advanced Study

Audi, Robert, and Nicholas Wolterstorff. *Religion in the Public Square: The Place of Religious Convictions in Political Debate*. Lanham, MD: Rowman & Littlefield, 1997. In this intelligent and insightful book, Audi and Wolterstorff debate two competing views on the role of religion in the public sphere.

Maclure, Jocelyn, and Charles Taylor. *Secularism and Freedom of Conscience*. Translated by Jane Marie Todd. Cambridge, MA: Harvard University Press, 2011. Just what is secularism, and how should it relate to religious diversity? Maclure and Taylor offer a brief but cogent discussion of these questions with attention to concrete cases.

Paul VI, Pope. "*Dignitatis Humanae*: Declaration on Religious Freedom." December 7, 1965. http://www.vatican.va/archive /hist_councils/ii_vatican_council/documents/vat-ii_decl_196

51207_dignitatis-humanae_en.html. This document from the
Second Vatican Council launched the Catholic Church's official
support for religious freedom.

Volf, Miroslav. "Mindsets of Respect, Regimes of Respect." In
Flourishing: Why We Need Religion in a Globalized World,
97–136. New Haven: Yale University Press, 2016. This chapter
discusses what it means to respect not only adherents of other
religions but, in a qualified way, those religions themselves,
notwithstanding our disagreement with their central claims.
It argues also that in addition to fostering "cultures of respect"
we need corresponding "regimes of respect."

PART 3

CHARACTER

21

COURAGE

Father Stan

They came to "disappear" Father Stan in the dark of night on July 28, 1981. When he refused to go with them quietly, the men shot him to death there in the parish house. Just seven months before, Stanley Rother had gone home to the United States, reluctantly leaving the village of Santiago Atitlán, Guatemala, after learning that his name was on one of the many death lists that the military dictatorship and its supporters used to organize a murderous campaign against their perceived enemies. Father Stan had drawn the ire of the government for supporting the poor and powerless of Santiago. He helped found the town's first hospital and an artisan cooperative. He championed education for local children. He worked to improve the town's meager infrastructure, even personally helping install electricity at several houses. He spoke and translated the Bible into the local Tzutujil language. But most offensively to the government, he opened the doors of the church to those seeking refuge from the army, so that they could not be kidnapped quietly from their homes.[1]

Father Stan tried to adjust to life back in Oklahoma, but his love for the people of Santiago left him yearning to share their struggle and suffering. Knowing full well the risk, he returned to Guatemala in time to celebrate Christ's death and resurrection with his congregation during Holy Week. Less than four months later, the congregation was mourning his death. The war that had claimed his and so many other lives took another fifteen years to end. The scars still mar Santiago. There are poverty and violence. There are alcoholism and PTSD. And there is still a bullet hole in the parish house floor. But the works of love that Father Stan helped lead are still bearing fruit too. The hospital that Father Stan founded is still in operation. Students from poor families who went to school with scholarships from Father Stan's program have gone on to become teachers, human rights lawyers, and mayor of Santiago. And people still come to the little room with the bullet hole to pay their respects and pray.

Father Stan embodied political courage. Despite the risk to his life, he wrote parables of the kingdom of God with his own life. He had the Christlike courage to see and do what was right for individuals and for the common good.

Courage and Love

Of all the virtues, courage is perhaps the one most obviously suited for public life. It sounds heroic, right at home in the theater of big, consequential endeavors. In fact, the fit is so good that, observing acts of extraordinary courage on the public stage, we might be misled about the nature of true courage. It's easy to think of courage mainly in terms of bravery and fearlessness. We picture the soldier who rushes into battle seemingly without concern for the overwhelming odds against him, like the cavalrymen in Alfred Lord Tennyson's "The Charge of the Light Brigade." The image isn't wrong, but it isn't exactly right either. It misses an essential aspect of courage, at least in a Christian account of it: its connection to love. Rebecca Konyndyk DeYoung defines courage, following the North African church father Augustine, as "love readily bearing all things for the sake of the object beloved."[2] Viewed in this light, bravery alone isn't enough for courage. "Without love," DeYoung writes, "all the bravery in the world is mere gritted teeth."[3] If loveless bravery is "mere grit," even vainglorious grit, perhaps we could call the courage of love "true grit."[4] Jesus displayed such courage. He boldly chastised influential religious leaders for the burdens they imposed on the people (Luke 11:45–46), and out of love for God and his people, he "set his face to go to Jerusalem," despite knowing what awaited him there (Luke 9:51). Father Stan's courage, too, was in the service of love. When asked why he was persecuted and murdered, two of his parishioners replied, "For loving the people here and helping the poor."[5] We are courageous when we take risks for the good of those we love.

Love isn't just the goal of courage; it is also its source. "Perfect love casts out fear," we read in 1 John 4:18. It's not that a courageous person doesn't *feel* afraid. When you're confronted with risks, your heartbeat might quicken and your hands begin to sweat, and yet you are courageous if you do what love bids you nevertheless. When we indulge in fear and let it determine our actions, when we let it creep into our very stance toward the world so that we act out of fear even without feeling fear, then we have lost both courage and love; or rather, our love sits paralyzed, unable to do the good that needs to be done. As love strengthens and grows, however, courage grows with it, and even feelings of fear begin to fade. As we accept risks to ourselves out of concern for others, fear doesn't grip us as often or as hard as it used to. Love has made us courageous.

Courage in Action

Terrible situations like the Guatemalan civil war throw into stark relief the need for courage in public engagement. But mostly we need courage in more ordinary situations.

- *We need courage when we know the right judgment would imply a policy that would cost us something.* Imagine that you had been benefiting from an unfair, gerrymandered school-district map that gathered all the kids from the well-off neighborhoods into one or two high-performing schools while the rest of the district's children attended dysfunctional schools. You might find yourself looking for ways to justify that unfair map.

- *We need courage when people around us—family members, powers that be, "everyone"—overwhelmingly support injustice.*[6] A member of a segregationist family and church in the 1950s, for instance, would be under immense pressure not to "betray" the community by insisting that segregation was wrong.

- *We need courage when our communities are hardly even considering important convictions that ought to be guiding them.* For instance, when the rhetoric of security, economic cost, and even outright xenophobia dominates public discussion about refugees from the war in Syria, it takes courage to stand up for our moral obligation to care for refugees (see chap. 15). Other convictions we have discussed in this book might also fall into this category.

- *We also need courage to make judgments and undertake actions at all, for in doing so we risk being wrong and doing wrong.* We are imperfect people whose knowledge is inherently limited, so even when we have conquered fear and are convinced that we have rendered judgment truthfully, we might be mistaken. Recognizing our fallibility calls for humility, as we discuss in chapter 22. It also calls for courage. If we are afraid to act because we might be wrong, we will be paralyzed and will by default make the judgment that it is fine for things to continue just as they are. Our first courage is the very fact of accepting responsibility, making judgments, and acting.

Courage and Risk

We tend to think of courage as a person risking *herself* for the sake of someone else or a greater good. In public life, the risks can indeed be to ourselves, as the examples of Father Stan and Dr. King demonstrate. But our actions also involve risks to others—in King's case, risk to his family and the entire civil rights movement. Or to return to an example above, if we advocate for a revision of the school-district map, we risk our children and those of our neighbors having worse educational opportunities than they otherwise would have. Many political actions even involve risks for future generations. If we support government deficit spending now, we implicitly accept the risk of default on behalf of our grandchildren. Similarly, if we reject environmental regulations, we accept the risk that future generations will inherit a radically degraded planet.

Many situations involve risks no matter what we do. Sociologists Ulrich Beck and Anthony Giddens have argued that developments in modern technology, economics, and government have increased the number of risks that we (mostly implicitly) take on and impose on others. They contend that we live in a "risk society"—a society in which our actions create risks we cannot calculate or do not even recognize as risks.[7]

The risk involved in public engagement varies widely depending on the situation. It runs from the relatively less serious, such as losing the esteem of an influential acquaintance, to the extremely grave, such as suffering violence and death or seriously harming others. When risks are weighty and involve harm to others, we might wonder if courage is desirable at all. Shouldn't caution prevail? Perhaps. But consider the consequences of inaction. Failing to act rightly risks letting wrong occur without resistance. In many cases, inaction can make us directly complicit in injustice. Imagine, for example, a police officer in Selma, Alabama, in 1965 who lacked the courage to disobey an order to beat the peaceful civil rights marchers. Moreover, when considering the big-picture risks involved in so many decisions about the common good today, lack of courage could easily lead to paralysis. We might simply abdicate responsibility and let things take their course, wherever that might lead. Sometimes there's no good option; both courage and caution seem to have unacceptable downsides.

To live responsibly with the tension between courage and caution, we need to recognize that courage must operate in tandem with the virtue of prudence or wisdom. In traditional theological accounts of the virtues, such as Thomas Aquinas's, cowardice isn't the only vice opposed to courage. There are also what he calls in Latin *intimiditas* and *audacia*.[8] The first means not feeling fear at all when we reasonably should, and the second means acting rashly, disregarding fear for no good reason. Courage involves prudent assessment of the risks we face, reasonable respect for their seriousness, and wise judgment regarding when to accept them and act in spite of them. It's a challenging task, but we're called to it, because without courage we cannot love well, especially in the public arena.

Resources for Further Reflection

Introductory Reading

Bader-Saye, Scott, and Chris Keller. "Following Jesus in a Political Climate of Fear: An Interview with Scott Bader-Saye." *The Other Journal*, October 16, 2008. http://theotherjournal.com/2008/10/16 /following-jesus-in-a-political-climate-of-fear-an-interview-with -scott-bader-saye/. Bader-Saye discusses the importance of courage if Christians are to be faithful amid the political and economic fears of our times. See also Bader-Saye's book *Following Jesus in a Culture of Fear* (Grand Rapids: Brazos, 2007).

Bonhoeffer, Dietrich. "Civil Courage and Public Responsibility." *Public Theology*, September 2009. http://www.pubtheo.com /page.asp?pid=1356. Imprisoned for treason against the Nazi regime, Bonhoeffer reflects on the importance of courage for responsible political action.

DeYoung, Rebecca Konyndyk. "Courage." In *Being Good: Christian Virtues for Everyday Life*, edited by Michael W. Austin and R. Douglas Geivett, 145–66. Grand Rapids: Eerdmans, 2012. DeYoung argues that Christian courage encompasses not only acts of daring bravery but also acts of courageous endurance and links the two through the priority of love.

King, Martin Luther, Jr. "Antidotes for Fear." In *The Strength to Love*, 119–32. Minneapolis: Fortress, 2010. King discusses the importance of courage, together with love and faith, in overcoming fear in the context of social transformation.

Advanced Study

Hauerwas, Stanley, and Charles Pinches. "Courage Exemplified." In *Christians among the Virtues*, 149–65. Notre Dame, IN: University of Notre Dame Press, 1997. This essay argues that Christianity transforms the virtue of courage by shifting the paradigm case from the soldier to the martyr.

Porter, Jean. "The Affective Virtues." In *The Recovery of Virtue: The Relevance of Aquinas for Christian Ethics*, 100–123. Louisville: Westminster John Knox, 1990. Porter provides a detailed account of courage through an analysis of its role in a flourishing human life.

Ruether, Rosemary Radford. "Courage as a Christian Virtue." *Cross Currents* 33, no. 1 (Spring 1983): 8–16. This essay puts Christian courage in historical perspective and argues for its continuing importance if the church is to be a prophetic community in the contemporary world.

Thomas Aquinas. *Summa Theologiae* II-II.123–40. http://www.newadvent.org/summa/. Aquinas defines courage as the virtue that rationally curbs fear and moderates daring. See especially II-II.123–28.

22

HUMILITY

"Do nothing from selfish ambition or vainglory, but in *humility of mind* regard others as better than yourselves. Let each of you look not to your own interests, but to the interests of others" (Phil. 2:3–4, emphasis added).[1] Having given this command, Paul then grounds it in the story of Christ. "Let the same *mind* be in you that was in Christ Jesus, who, though he was in the form of God, did not regard equality with God as something to be exploited, but emptied himself, taking the form of a slave, being born in human likeness. And being found in human form, he humbled himself and became obedient to the point of death—even death on a cross" (Phil. 2:5–8, emphasis added).

Humility is clearly a Christian virtue—perhaps even the signature Christian virtue. It stands at odds with many prevalent cultural sensibilities today, as it did with the dominant ethic of glory and honor in Christ's day.[2] Humility appears especially out of place in the world of politics, where nations and their leaders vie with one another for glory and gain. And yet the New Testament calls us to be humble as Christ was humble. Heeding this call would profoundly transform our public engagement.

What Is Humility?

It's common to think that humility means having a low opinion of oneself. This idea of humility, however, runs into a significant problem. It seems to demand that if someone were truly impressive, she would have to overlook or deliberately ignore that fact. She would have to have a false view of herself. But how could a virtue depend on falsehood?[3] An alternative approach tries to save the low-opinion account of humility by arguing that because all humans are sinful, we all have good reason to hold ourselves in low esteem. On this view, nothing we do could ever truly deserve esteem, so we all ought to be humble.[4] From a Christian perspective, however, neither of these views can work (at least on its own), because neither can give a good account of Jesus Christ's humility.

The Scriptures give us no reason to think that Christ had a low opinion of himself. Indeed, they give us good reason to think that would be impossible. Jesus is the incarnate Word, the Son of God, and so is worthy of worship and adoration. He is also the only human without sin (Heb. 4:15), so his humility can't be grounded in acknowledgment of his own sin. Far more than for any other human, Christ could hold a low opinion of himself only through carefully maintained ignorance or out-and-out self-deception, neither of which is fitting for the one who is himself the truth (John 14:6).

Perhaps, then, Christ's humility consists in the fact that he does not think *too* highly of himself. There's nothing problematic about this idea, except that Scripture gives a different account of Christ's humility. In Philippians 2:5–8, Christ does seem to know that he is "in the form of God" and equal with God, but that accurate knowledge isn't what makes him humble. Rather, he is humble because, despite his equality with God, he willingly took on humanity and even an incredibly shameful human death. He set aside his rightful status for the sake of God's mission and the good of others. A person with Christlike humility doesn't regard her status as a reason not to do what love requires. No good deed is beneath her dignity. Indeed, while she might on one level know what her status is, she doesn't think of it at all when commitment to follow Christ gives her a job to do. She thinks of the task at hand.

This suggests that humility is more about *not thinking of yourself too much* than *not thinking too much of yourself*.[5] Humility isn't a matter of self-appraisal. Instead, it's a matter of not worrying about how great you are or whether other people give due deference to your greatness. It follows that humility doesn't dwell on comparisons of status. We see this in Christ's readiness to talk theology with a Samaritan woman (John 4:1–42), hang out with tax collectors (Mark 2:14–15), and wash his disciples' feet (John 13:3–14). Jesus just doesn't seem concerned about who is better than whom, more or less worthy of praise or recognition, although he is certainly ready to praise those whom others would tend to disregard, whether they be a poor widow (Mark 12:41–44) or a commander in the occupying imperial army (Luke 7:1–9). Christ is devoted above all to God's mission in the world. All else, including his reputation with the big shots of his day, is subsidiary.

For those of us who aren't the eternal Son of God, disregard for our own glory out of commitment to the kingdom of God leads inevitably to a keen awareness of our own limits. Awed by the scope and grandeur of the kingdom and the creation that it transforms, we see our own relative smallness. We know that not every good stream runs through our lives, that there are whole oceans of goodness with which we haven't the faintest acquaintance. At the same time, grieved by the brokenness of creation and how unlike the kingdom it remains, we see the limits of our own goodness with distressing clarity. We know ourselves, like the tax collector in Jesus's parable, as sinners (Luke 18:9–14). While humility isn't about self-appraisal, it does foster candid self-assessment.

Humility thus has two aspects: (1) unconcern for our own glory and status out of commitment to Christ and his mission and (2) sober awareness of our limits. The two go together. Not only does commitment to the kingdom give rise to awareness of our limits, but humble awareness of our limits readies us to follow Christ in pursuit of the kingdom. Stephen Cherry writes, "True humility is acutely and profoundly aware of the promise, the presence and the absence of the kingdom of God and the tension between them. And it is this awareness which makes it both self-forgetful and deeply passionate."[6] Humility clears away our preoccupation with being good enough and receiving recognition for our goodness and thus "allows us to present and offer ourselves, profoundly limited as we are, in the cause of God's mission."[7]

Humble Public Engagement

At first glance, humility doesn't seem—like courage—to be at home on the public stage. On closer examination, however, we see that it is vitally important for following Christ in the public arena. Humility keeps us from getting caught up in the mad scramble for attention, reputation, and status that characterizes so much of contemporary public life. The whole process of a modern electoral campaign, for instance, boils down to candidates "selling" themselves to constituencies, striving for the highest name recognition and the best approval ratings. Candidates carefully craft their "brands" and tailor every word and gesture to match them. The media focus on the horse race of campaigns more than the issues that are at stake. Politicians and pundits treat governing like a zero-sum game, where admitting that the other side has done even the least bit of good undermines one's standing and achievement. Unlike such self-promotion, humility focuses on the tasks at hand and welcomes foretastes of the kingdom wherever it finds them, even among our erstwhile opponents.

Almost by definition it's hard to identify people who manifest this kind of political humility. We can catch a glimpse of it, however, in the life of someone like George C. Marshall, the chief of staff of the US Army during World War II and, in the aftermath of the war, the architect of the European Recovery Program, better known as the Marshall Plan. Since Marshall had developed the Allied strategy for the liberation of Western Europe, he appeared to be first in line to be appointed general over the Allied troops in Europe. Marshall, however, refused to ask for the position or even admit to President Roosevelt that he wanted it. He wanted the president to make the decision with only the good of the Allied war effort, and not Marshall's desire for such an important field command, in mind. Roosevelt decided he needed Marshall to stay in Washington and chose Dwight D. Eisenhower for the post instead.[8]

Politicians and generals, however, aren't the only ones who need this sort of humility. In today's hyperactive attention-economy, all but the most anonymous public engagement has the potential to bring with it not only local recognition but also widespread fame or notoriety. Humility puts aside considerations of how we'll look—of what the tweets would say and how the viral video would play—and frees us to just be faithful. In addition, since people tend to identify with their countries, the dynamics of status seeking and reputation maintenance can distort our stances toward international relations. Excessive concern for national honor, for instance, can lead us to think that violence is necessary in order to defend it, that we must answer perceived slights or insults with hostility. Humility in such a case is the strength to put faithfulness to Christ above national prestige.

Humility's second aspect—sober awareness of our limits—also has far-reaching implications for public engagement. None of us is an expert in all the areas where judgments about the common good are required. None of us has all the right information. Even if we did, none of us is so virtuous that we would always do the right thing with it. Acknowledging these limits keeps us from the hubris of thinking we have it all figured out and others should just get with the program. Humility opens us to the possibility of new insights from unexpected places. It encourages actual dialogue, rather than shouting matches. It spurs us to the self-scrutiny that can reduce the chances of reckless mistakes. Imagine what a little more sober understanding of the limits of what American military power could accomplish might have done in 2003. The disaster of the Iraq war, with its rivers of blood, streams of refugees, and immense waste of resources, could have been avoided!

The two aspects of humility come together to foster one of the rarest but most important political virtues: the willingness to admit when we (individually or collectively) have been wrong, to repent, and to change our course regardless of what it means for our reputations. Humble readiness to acknowledge that mistakes and wrongdoing are not just "out there" but also "in here" is indispensable for faithful public discipleship. It promotes truthfulness and opens the door to reconciliation.

Resources for Further Reflection

Introductory Reading

Baehr, Jason. "How Does Humility Contribute to Strength?" *Big Questions Online*, December 10, 2013. https://www.big questionsonline.com/content/how-does-humility-contribute -strength. Baehr makes the counterintuitive argument that acknowledgment of our limits and failures is integral to strength.

Cherry, Stephen. *Barefoot Disciple: Walking the Way of Passionate Humility*. London: Continuum, 2011. Cherry offers a profound meditation on humility as self-forgetful, passionate pursuit of God's kingdom and on ways of living that might open us up to becoming more humble.

Dickson, John. *Humilitas*. Grand Rapids: Zondervan, 2011. Dickson provides a very accessible historical overview of humility in the Hebrew Bible, the New Testament, and Greco-Roman culture and asks how humility can shape our understanding of leadership.

Pinsent, Andrew. "Humility." In *Being Good: Christian Virtues for Everyday Living*, edited by Michael W. Austin and R. Douglas

Geivett, 242–64. Grand Rapids: Eerdmans, 2012. Working from
an analysis of pride to a definition of humility, Pinsent lays
out a somewhat different account of humility than ours and
discusses the central significance of humility in specifically
Christian moral thought.

Advanced Study

Button, Mark. "'A Monkish Kind of Virtue'? For and against Humility." *Political Theory* 33 (2005): 840–68. Button argues that
humility is a paradigmatically democratic virtue and helpfully
overviews modern philosophical critiques of humility.

Herdt, Jennifer A. "Christian Humility, Courtly Civility, and the
Code of the Streets." *Modern Theology* 25 (2009): 541–57.
Herdt intriguingly relates New Testament texts to Renaissance
codes of conduct and contemporary anthropological accounts
of inner-city life and shows the surprising relevance of humility
for contemporary contexts.

Roberts, Robert C., and W. Jay Wood. "Humility." In *Intellectual
Virtues: An Essay in Regulative Epistemology*, 236–56. Oxford:
Oxford University Press, 2007. Roberts and Wood engage in a
lucid exploration of humility's relation to the vices of vanity
and arrogance.

Wengst, Klaus. *Humility: Solidarity of the Humiliated*. Philadelphia: Fortress, 1988. In this clear assessment of humility in
Greco-Roman thought, the Hebrew Bible, and early Christian
texts, Wengst claims that humility is part of the liberation of
the oppressed, rather than an instrument of their oppression.

23

JUSTICE

"The kingdom of God is not food and drink," Paul writes to the church at Rome, "but justice and peace and joy in the Holy Spirit" (Rom. 14:17).[1] As this and many other biblical passages emphasize, justice is central to the Christian faith and therefore to Christian public engagement. The good news of the kingdom is, in great part, that God's justice will make an end to all the injustice prevalent in the world. The psalmist writes about that day:

> Let the sea roar, and all that fills it;
>   the world and those who live in it.
> Let the floods clap their hands;
>   let the hills sing together for joy
> at the presence of the LORD, for he is coming
>   to judge the earth.
> He will judge the world with righteousness,
>   and the peoples with equity.
>
> (Ps. 98:7–9)

Since God rules with justice, whenever justice prevails in our political societies, they anticipate God's coming kingdom in a real, even if broken, way. It's not surprising, therefore, that the Bible is full of commands to do justice (e.g., Deut. 16:18–20; Isa. 1:17; Amos 5:15), lamentations over and condemnations of the injustice of the current political order (e.g., Isa. 5:8–10; 10:1–5; Amos 5:10–11; Mic. 3:9–12), and praise for the rare ruler who is just (e.g., Deut. 33:21; 2 Sam. 23:3–4). Christian faith yearns for and seeks the sort of society that reflects God's justice.

What Is Justice?

As the biblical passages mentioned indicate, justice is in part a matter of social structures and specific actions. That's how we generally think of justice today. We have the "criminal justice system" and, in the world of superheroes, the "Justice League," both of which seek to bring the perpetrators of offense "to justice." But justice isn't entirely about arranging things well in the world. It's also about the sort of people we are, what sort of character and dispositions we have. This is justice as a virtue, less popular today but no less important an aspect of justice than these others. For the justice of a society depends considerably on the justice of its members (just as the justice of its members is influenced by the justice or lack of it in society).

Historically, when Christians answered the question of what it means to be a just person, they often quoted the Roman lawyer Ulpian (ca. 170–223): "Justice is a steady and enduring will to render to everyone his right."[2] Justice is the virtue of being disposed to give people what is owed to them—whether that is punishment or a reward or simply leaving them in peace. Justice, understood as giving people their due, is a central political virtue.

But there is another sense in which the Bible uses the term *justice*. It goes beyond what we owe people and includes what God commands that we should give them nonetheless—forgiveness, for instance. The word *righteousness* is sometimes used to designate this second sense of justice, and it includes fulfilling all the demands of love. Righteous persons are those who love God above all things and love neighbors as themselves. Justice (giving people their due) is not opposed to righteousness but is part of it; we cannot be righteous if we fail to give people wages they deserve. Righteousness (giving people more than their due) is not opposed to justice but is a realization of what it aims at; I am not unjust, for example, if I cover an experimental treatment that someone's insurance does not cover.

The Public Good of Justice

As a public virtue, justice is important above all in four regards. First, the stress on justice excludes a common way of understanding democratic politics, the "interest adjudication" model. On this view, the political process is meant to provide a framework in which individuals and groups can advocate for their own private interests. Democratic institutions serve to make sure the competition happens as fairly as possible. Justice, however, seeks not to maximize what I receive but to ensure that all receive their due. It displaces my interest from the center of my concern and places equity there instead.

Second, the stress on justice draws attention to the many goods we share in common with others. It is easy to think of our personal good as more or less independent from that of others, but in fact it depends intrinsically on a slew of important goods that we can have only by holding them in common with others. Think of roads, schools, potable water, food-safety requirements, stable currency, clean air, and so on. Even when we recognize our dependence on these shared goods, we often tend to appropriate them for ourselves to the exclusion of others. We might, for instance, diligently lobby the city to repair the roads along our commute, while ignoring the disrepair of streets in neighborhoods we don't visit. Justice militates against such co-optation of common goods for private purposes.

Third, commitment to justice counters the temptation to let the laws of the land determine our judgments about what is right.

Some laws are unjust, as Isaiah says when he declares in the name of the Lord, "Woe to those who make *unjust laws*, to those who issue oppressive decrees" (Isa. 10:1 NIV, emphasis added). Justice is the measure of laws, not the other way around. The British abolitionists led by William Wilberforce (1759–1833) exemplified justice's appeal to a standard beyond mere legal requirement in their campaigns against the slave trade and slavery in the British Empire. Slaveholders complained that abolition would violate their property rights, but Wilberforce insisted in reply that the plantation owners held slaves "by no right that is not opposed to nature, reason, justice, and religion."[3] One of Wilberforce's collaborators, a member of Parliament named Thomas Fowell Buxton (1786–1845), remarkably demonstrated the virtue of justice. He argued fervently against the institution of slavery ("a rank, naked, flagrant, undisguised injustice"), and yet he granted that because British law had licensed the injustice of slavery, the slaveholders might have some "claim against the British Nation," even though they had no right to hold slaves.[4] Just people give what is due even to their opponents and enemies.

Fourth, stress on justice counters the human tendency to show partiality toward the powerful, a wrongdoing that draws special ire from the Hebrew prophets (see Isa. 1:23; 10:2). The one God of all humans is just and "shows no partiality" (Acts 10:34). Many pressures, however, push us to make exceptions for the exceptional. There's the chance that they might return the favor one day, or more darkly, that they might punish us for not giving them their way. These prospects threaten to blur our vision. We need the virtue of justice in order to cut through the glare of fame, wealth, and power and see what really counts when determining what is due.

Things We Are Due

Justice gives others their due. But just what is due to people? One of Jesus's parables suggests an understanding of due patterned on

God's character that is markedly different from our usual sense of justice.

> The kingdom of heaven is like a landowner who went out early in the morning to hire laborers for his vineyard. After agreeing with the laborers for the usual daily wage, he sent them into his vineyard. When he went out about nine o'clock, he saw others standing idle in the marketplace; and he said to them, "You also go into the vineyard, and *I will pay you whatever is right.*" So they went. When he went out again about noon and about three o'clock, he did the same. And about five o'clock he went out and found others standing around; and he said to them, "Why are you standing here idle all day?" They said to him, "Because no one has hired us." He said to them, "You also go into the vineyard." When evening came, the owner of the vineyard said to his manager, "Call the laborers and give them their pay, beginning with the last and then going to the first." When those hired about five o'clock came, each of them received the usual daily wage. Now when the first came, *they thought they would receive more*; but each of them also received the usual daily wage. And when they received it, they grumbled against the landowner, saying, "These last worked only one hour, and *you have made them equal to us* who have borne the burden of the day and the scorching heat." But he replied to one of them, "Friend, I am doing you no wrong; did you not agree with me for the usual daily wage? Take *what belongs to you* and go; I choose to give to this last the same as I give to you. Am I not allowed to do what I choose with *what belongs to me*? Or are you envious because I am generous?" (Matt. 20:1–15, emphasis added)

The complaining early arrivers are upset that the owner doesn't recognize and reward their greater effort and achievement with a greater wage than the latecomers receive. They complain about the equality that the owner's actions create between such apparently unequal laborers. The landowner, however, denies that he is doing them any wrong. The wage they agreed on, he says, belongs to them. That is their due. Higher pay based only on their longer workday is not. The text in turn implies that it is *right* for the latecomers to receive the wage they do ("I will pay you whatever is right"). According to common expectations, the owner is being arbitrarily generous, but his words suggest that he is only paying the later arrivers what is right—what he *ought* to give them and even in some sense what is due to them. Those still waiting for work at five o'clock are *due* the opportunity to work and to earn enough to secure the necessities of life (see chap. 7). This *particular* landowner, however, doesn't *owe* that to them until he, acting in accordance with justice as righteousness, hires them.

There are no hard and fast rules for computing what is due to whom in any concrete situation. Even Jesus's parable doesn't provide a simple formula that will guarantee we correctly identify what justice requires. Though it gives us good reason to think that God's justice involves care for all, its lesson is not the simple conclusion: "Justice requires that we always give everyone the same wages." Determining what is just requires practical wisdom and faithful discernment. Still, this parable and the biblical witness more generally suggest some broad guidelines for determining what is due to whom.

The vineyard owner seems to have believed that the laborers left standing around without work until five in the afternoon are being deprived of something they are due—namely, the opportunity to work and earn the resources they need to survive. A purely competitive logic of the labor market would say that these stragglers are likely the least efficient workers, so their due is precisely what they have gotten: a day without a job. Today, many assume that it is just to pay workers what a competitive market determines is their due: as little as they are willing to work for. A Christian understanding of justice, while not denying the validity of market determinations of due, denies their monopoly. There are various different forms of due, some of which might look quite "unfair" from a market standpoint.

We can explain at least part of the variety of kinds of due by the fact that there are different sources of due. In some cases I am due something based on an accomplishment of mine—say, a high school diploma for having passed the right set of courses. In others, the source is a promise that someone has made to me—say, the fidelity of a spouse who has made a marital vow to faithfulness. In still others, it's simply my need that establishes what I am due—say, food if I am starving. To be truly just, we must honor the multiplicity of sources of due, rather than treat one, such as merit, as the only legitimate one.

Resources for Further Reflection

Introductory Reading

Keenan, James F. "Justice." In *Virtues for Ordinary Christians*, 64–69. New York: Sheed & Ward, 1996. Keenan argues that justice is about not merely legality but also the skills and habits needed for common life in society.

Slote, Michael. "Justice as a Virtue." *Stanford Encyclopedia of Philosophy*. July 22, 2014. http://plato.stanford.edu/entries /justice-virtue/. Slote provides a useful overview of historical and contemporary philosophical treatments of the virtue of justice.

Stassen, Glen H., and David P. Gushee. "Justice." In *Kingdom Ethics: Following Jesus in Contemporary Context*, 345–65. Downers Grove, IL: InterVarsity, 2003. Stassen and Gushee develop a biblically grounded picture of justice by reading the life of Jesus in light of the Hebrew prophets.

Wadell, Paul J. "Reimagining the World: Justice." In *Happiness and the Christian Moral Life: An Introduction to Christian Ethics*, 225–50. Lanham, MD: Rowman & Littlefield, 2012. Wadell argues that justice is the center of the Christian moral life and considers the ways in which conversion from injustice to justice requires renewed ways of thinking and seeing the world.

Advanced Study

Harrison, Beverly Wildung. "The Dream of a Common Language: Toward a Normative Theory of Justice in Christian Ethics." In *Justice in the Making: Feminist Social Ethics*, edited by Elizabeth M. Bounds, Pamela K. Brubaker, Marilyn J. Legge, and Rebecca Todd Peters, 14–29. Louisville: Westminster John Knox, 2004. Harrison argues for a radical conception of justice as rightly related community, and she shows how a Christian feminist social ethic can illuminate justice.

Porter, Jean. "Justice." In *The Recovery of Virtue: The Relevance of Aquinas for Christian Ethics*, 124–54. Louisville: Westminster John Knox, 1990. Porter argues that justice corrects the will so that the individual's good aligns with the common good without subordinating one to the other.

Thomas Aquinas. *Summa Theologiae* II-II.57–122 (especially 57–61). http://www.newadvent.org/summa/. This is Aquinas's classic treatment of the virtue of justice as "a habit whereby a man renders to each one his due by a consistent and perpetual will."

Wolterstorff, Nicholas. *Justice: Rights and Wrongs*. Princeton: Princeton University Press, 2008. This important book offers a theological grounding for human rights and argues that justice is a matter of inherent rights and their corresponding obligations.

24

RESPECT

In December 2014, Hillary Clinton gave an address at Georgetown University. Speaking on foreign policy, she advocated an approach that would include, among other things, "showing respect even for one's enemies."[1] This phrase sparked intense criticism.[2] Many commentators simply assumed that it would be absurd to respect America's enemies. Even some political supporters objected to Clinton's language. Former Democratic congresswoman Jane Harman said, "I think we need to respect those who live in the Middle East who are devout Muslims and who think that our policies are wrong. . . . I don't think we have to respect members of terror groups ever."[3] The debate reminds us not just of the importance of respect but of unresolved questions about it. What is respect? Whom should we respect and why? Whom, if anyone, should we disrespect or even despise?

Two Kinds of Respect

Respect, defined generally, is the acknowledgment of someone's worth. Certain kinds of worth are *due* our acknowledgment; it would be wrong not to respect such worth.[4] But it would also be wrong to acknowledge worth where there isn't any. If you disrespect someone's worth, you aren't giving that person her due and are wronging her; if you respect someone lacking worth, you are declaring him to be better than he is, possibly even whitewashing his faults. That's respect in general.

It is crucial, though, to distinguish two kinds of respect. The moral philosopher Stephen Darwall calls them *appraisal respect* and *recognition respect*.[5] Appraisal respect is positive evaluation of somebody's achievements or virtues. It's the sort of respect you might express by saying, "As a Jets/Barca fan, I root against the Patriots/Real Madrid, but I still have to respect Tom Brady's/Christiano Ronaldo's talent on the field," or, "I respect the courage you showed by blowing the whistle on the unethical behavior going on in your company." In contrast, recognition respect is elicited by the worth someone has simply by being what she is. We might respect the president of a country in virtue of the office she holds even if we don't deem her performance in office worthy of respect.

Much of our talk about respect—whether in business, science, and technology or in sports, civic engagement, and religion—focuses on appraisal respect. And rightly so. We honor people for their achievements and their admirable character traits. This is the kind of respect that the good and faithful servant received from the master, according to one of Jesus's parables (Matt. 25:23). It would be abhorrent to respect the moral character of militants of the so-called Islamic State, the point Clinton's detractors may have been making. Inversely, it would be unjust to fail to respect the character of the Dalai Lama.

Appraisal respect comes with a danger, though. It lurks in the values we apply to determine what is worthy of respect and what is not. The gospel has its own standards of what counts as notable and what sort of character is respectable, and these often run against the prevailing spirit of today's success-oriented cultures. Jesus appraised the widow's mite (Mark 12:41–44; Luke 21:1–4) and the tax collector's cry for help (Luke 18:9–14) more highly than the gold of the rich and the boast of the Pharisee. And Paul proclaims, "God chose what is foolish in the world to shame the wise; God chose what is weak in the world to shame the strong; God chose what is low and despised in the world, things that are not, to reduce to nothing things that are" (1 Cor. 1:27–28). As followers of Christ, we must hold up gospel values as the measure of true worth and be on guard lest we judge guided by prevalent but perverted norms.

Even more importantly, appraisal respect should not be the main basis for our treatment of others. Rather, recognition respect should be, specifically the recognition respect due human beings on account of their humanity. Sometimes we give recognition respect to someone as the holder of an office (e.g., president) or as having a certain relationship to us (e.g., parent). We can interpret the command in 1 Peter 2:17 to "honor the emperor" as having to do with this kind of respect. But there's also a form of recognition respect that acknowledges the fundamental worth of someone simply as a human being. It's this sort of respect that Christians are commanded to give when the same verse from 1 Peter says, "Honor *everyone*" (emphasis added). But *why* should we respect everyone? How *could* we respect everyone?

The philosopher Nicholas Wolterstorff has argued that a certain kind of love, which he calls "love as attachment," bestows worth on the beloved.[6] Attachment makes the Velveteen Rabbit so much more valuable than just any stuffed animal sitting unbought on the toy-store shelf. It is a special relationship that makes something valuable. God's love is that sort of love, so it gives people worth. And since God's love is universal—since there is no human being to whom God isn't attached and for whose salvation the Son of God didn't come into the world—*all* humans have inalienable worth. That worth demands recognition respect. And since the worth is universal, respect should be utterly indiscriminate. It should include everyone, no exceptions and no qualifications.

People earn appraisal respect; they are owed recognition respect just for being human.[7]

Appraisal respect and recognition respect are both active stances toward others, rather than mere feelings. They are not just our "internal" views about people but rather postures toward them that include thoughts, feelings, and actions; they affect the whole way we treat people. If you have respect for someone, you will act toward that person in a certain way. And then, going beyond the stance of respect is the virtue of respect*fulness*. Rather than an incidental stance that could come and go, it is the enduring disposition to respect rightly.

Respectfulness

Why is respectfulness, especially the disposition to have recognition respect, an important public virtue? Public life brings differences, disagreements, and often wrongdoings squarely to center stage and so poses obstacles to respect. Every society is divided by strong disagreements about the important issues of its common life, from tax policy to immigration. Further complicating the picture, most people today live in pluralistic societies with numerous ethnic, religious, and class groups. People with different and sometimes clashing visions of the good life have to negotiate how to live with one another. And to top it off, all political societies are marked by a history of injustices, injuries, and insults large and small—all of which make grievances and demands to redress them part of the everyday stuff of political life.

The conflictual character of public life in pluralistic societies often militates against both appraisal and recognition respect. It is tempting to disrespectfully prejudge people who take a different side than we do. We fail to see the value of their arguments or the praiseworthiness of their character because we discount them ahead of time as the "enemy." We thus fail to show appropriate appraisal respect. But appraisal disrespect slips all too easily into recognition disrespect. We go from thinking that someone's opinion is worthless or his character despicable to thinking that he, as a person, is unworthy of our regard. The danger is especially pronounced when wrongs have been committed. In the dark shadow that wrongdoing casts over the presumed wrongdoers, we often cease to see them as human persons and see instead only "criminals," "oppressors," "racists," or "terrorists,"[8] and, in extreme situations, "animals," "vermin," "cockroaches" that must be exterminated.

Disrespect of this kind hardly counts as conformity to the character of Christ, the Savior sent for all, whose Father's sun shines on the evil and the good (Matt. 5:45). Moreover, disrespecting others poisons public life and the search for the common good. Appraisal disrespect at the very least fosters acrimonious atmospheres with little hope for compromises or cooperation. If disrespect is pervasive, it whittles away at social trust. If it looks like everyone is judging others exclusively out of partisan motives, how can you trust anybody to speak the truth? Recognition disrespect can have even worse ramifications. Since it involves the refusal to see the other's value as a person, it effectively denies the other's humanity. Moreover, dehumanizing one's opponents dramatically facilitates violent and unjust treatment of them.[9] Political societies whose members consistently fail to give recognition respect are prone to violence and oppression.

Desmond Tutu, a man familiar both with long-standing social conflicts and with processes of reconciliation, has written, "It is only when we respect even our adversaries and see them not as ogres, dehumanized, demonized, but as fellow human beings deserving respect for their personhood and dignity, that we will conduct a discourse that just might prevent conflict."[10] No healthy public engagement for the common good is possible without unconditional respect for persons, especially when we are unable to respect their positions and practices. And no such respect will be possible without cultivation of the virtue of respectfulness.

Father Reid

The story of Father Alec Reid, a Catholic priest from Northern Ireland, exemplifies the power of respectfulness even in extreme political situations. Beginning in the late 1960s, Northern Ireland suffered thirty years of violence known as "the Troubles." Conflict over whether Northern Ireland should remain part of the United Kingdom (the Unionist position) or be part of the Republic of Ireland (the Republican position) erupted into clashes between Unionist paramilitaries, their Republican counterparts, and the British security forces.

Few people did as much as Father Reid to facilitate the dialogues that finally led to the end of the Troubles with the Good Friday Agreement in 1998. Over the course of more than a decade, Reid arranged meetings between the mainstream Unionist Party and the radical Sinn Féin (the political wing of the Irish Republican Army, or IRA), as well as governing parties from the Republic of Ireland; he relayed communications when meetings weren't possible; and he was one of two clergymen entrusted with verifying the IRA's destruction of its weapons as part of the peace accord. Reid was able to do this delicate work because he had the trust of all parties involved, and he had their trust in great part because he respected them all. Even when he condemned a group's methods or aims, he never ceased to engage its members in respectful dialogue.

Reid's commitment to respect every person shone forth particularly clearly one tragic March day in 1988. Two British soldiers in plainclothes, David Howes and Derek Wood, drove by the funeral procession of a Republican who had recently been killed by a Unionist gunman. Paramilitary members among the mourners dragged the soldiers from their car, stripped and beat them, and prepared to kill them. Reid, who was attending the funeral, tried unsuccessfully to intercede and then, when the men were shot, to resuscitate them. The militants considered the soldiers enemies of Reid's Catholic community and left their half-naked bodies lying in the street. Reid, however, refused to denigrate the murdered men's humanity. Instead, his face stained red from attempting mouth-to-mouth resuscitation, Reid acknowledged the slain soldiers' worth as beloved creatures of God by performing the last rites for them there on the bloody pavement. A photo of Reid's act became one of the defining images of the Northern Irish peace movement.

Not all of us will face times as extreme as the Troubles. Nor will we all display respectfulness as profound and tenacious as Alec Reid's. But we can aim for it, in hopes of witnessing to the worth of all people in light of God's love and contributing to more respectful political cultures.

Resources for Further Reflection

Introductory Reading

Boff, Leonardo. "Respect." In *Virtues for Another Possible World*, 143–58. Eugene, OR: Cascade Books, 2011. A prominent Latin American liberation theologian treats universal respect as one of the key virtues needed in the face of our present global and ecological crises.

Paul VI, Pope. *Gaudium et Spes*. December 7, 1965. http://www .vatican.va/archive/hist_councils/ii_vatican_council/documents /vat-ii_const_19651207_gaudium-et-spes_en.html. This document from the Second Vatican Council opens with a profound reflection on the dignity of the human person and the respect this dignity demands, both from individuals and from the social and political conditions in which a person lives.

Volf, Miroslav. "'Honor Everyone!' Christian Faith and the Culture of Universal Respect." In *Abraham's Children: Liberty and Tolerance in an Age of Religious Conflict*, edited by Kelly James Clark, 186–208. New Haven: Yale University Press, 2012. Working from the command in 1 Peter to honor everyone, this essay argues that Christian convictions entail universal respect and further explores the social and political ramifications of such respect.

―――. "Public Engagement." In *A Public Faith: How Followers of Christ Should Serve the Common Good*, 119–37. Grand Rapids: Brazos, 2011. This chapter focuses on the need for respect in political engagement with particular attention to the issue of religious disagreement.

Advanced Study

Darwall, Stephen L. "Two Kinds of Respect." *Ethics* 88 (1997): 36–49. Darwall explains and defends the distinction between appraisal respect and recognition respect.

Farley, Margaret A. "A Feminist Version of Respect for Persons." *Journal of Feminist Studies in Religion* 9 (1993): 183–98. Farley explores from a feminist perspective the question of the universally shared features in virtue of which human beings require respect.

Taylor, Charles. "The Politics of Recognition." In *Multicultural-ism: Examining the Politics of Recognition*, edited by Amy Gutmann, 25–74. Princeton: Princeton University Press, 1994. Taylor offers an account of the historical sources and current dynamics of the politics of equal respect as well as a partial defense of a particular form of multiculturalism.

Volf, Miroslav. "Mindsets of Respect, Regimes of Respect." In *Flourishing: Why We Need Religion in a Globalized World*, 97–136. New Haven: Yale University Press, 2016. A more developed version of "Honor Everyone!," this chapter extends the argument to other world religions and argues for a political regime of respect.

25

COMPASSION

Once, Jesus and the large crowd following him happened upon a funeral procession. The dead man, Luke tells us, "was his mother's only son, and she was a widow." The bereaved mother was accompanying her son's body, like his father's before it, to its resting place. She faced a bleak future of economic hardship and social isolation. Luke continues: "When the Lord saw her, he had compassion for her and said to her, 'Do not weep.' Then he came forward and touched the bier, and the bearers stood still. And he said, 'Young man, I say to you, rise!' The dead man sat up and began to speak, and Jesus gave him to his mother" (Luke 7:12–15). Amid such a stunning turn of events, we could easily overlook a little detail in Luke's text. Greeted with the scene, Jesus sees the grief-stricken mother, and, Luke observes, he has compassion for her. This verse isn't even close to the only time the Gospels mention Jesus's compassion (e.g., Matt. 9:36; 15:32; 20:34; Mark 8:2). Compassion clearly matters to Jesus. It is also indispensable for his followers' public engagement.

Compassion: A Political Virtue?

Compassion matters because humans aren't intellectual computing machines that take in data, perform calculations, spit out an optimal action plan, and then implement it. We are complex wholes—mishmashes of thoughts, emotions, desires, reflexes, and so forth. Right action does not simply follow right thought. It needs the help of emotions. But not any emotion will do. Some emotions lead us to betray our deep commitments; others drive us to override distorted beliefs and act better than we think. We need the right kind of emotions to act well in public. One such emotion is compassion, which is vital to living faithfully in a world marked by suffering and need. Without it, we're apt to pass by the wounded man on the street (Luke 10:30–32), or after having seen bodies ravaged by hunger on a TV screen, simply to return to our steak. Almost without exception, we need compassion to impel us to act swiftly and persistently to alleviate suffering and care for those in need. Moreover, compassion doesn't just spur action; it gives it a human touch. When we suffer or are in need, we mostly don't want merely to be the objects of a cold, calculated act of assistance. As our needs are being met, we also want to know that others identify with our situation. We seek compassion.

For disciples of Jesus Christ, who are committed to the marginalized, the suffering, and to those with unmet needs, compassion is particularly valuable because it is inherently oriented to precisely those people. The feeling of compassion is like a flare that captures our vision and indicates where we should focus attention. And since much of public life involves responses to suffering and deprivation, compassion is vital for faithful public engagement.

What Is Compassion?

Some people think of compassion as simply feeling others' pain. Compassion does involve feeling, but as an emotion and a virtue it is *more than* a feeling.[1] Theologians and philosophers have identified *three* aspects of virtuous compassion: feeling, thinking, and doing.[2]

The feeling aspect of compassion is love for the needy and suffering leading you to experience their pain as painful to you. It's not exactly feeling other people's pain *as yours*; rather, *their* pain prompts *your own* pain in response. Because you love them, their suffering matters to you and influences your feelings. The feeling aspect of compassion is inscribed right into the word itself. The Latin *compassio* means roughly "suffering/feeling with."

Strange as it might seem, compassion also involves *thinking*. Like all emotions and unlike mere feelings, compassion has certain beliefs or judgments built into it. For instance, it only makes sense for Jesus to have compassion for the widow of Nain if he knows something about the relation between mothers and sons and understands that she is suffering greatly from the loss of her son.

Finally and crucially, the virtue of compassion involves *doing* what you can to address suffering. It's striking to read the Gospel passages that talk about compassion. Every time the text says that Jesus has compassion on someone, it moves on immediately to his active care for the person or people in question. He cures the sick (Matt. 14:14; Mark 1:40–42). He multiplies loaves and fishes (Matt. 15:32–38; Mark 8:1–9). He touches blind men's eyes, and they see (Matt. 20:29–34). He says to a dead man, "Rise," and he rises (Luke 7:14–15). He commands his disciples to pray for more laborers to come and help in the harvest. And then he sends those disciples out to heal and deliver and proclaim the kingdom (Matt. 9:36–10:8). As Augustine put it, compassion is "a kind of fellow-feeling in our hearts for another's misery, *which compels us to come to his help* by every means in our power."[3] With true compassion, the question is not whether we'll take action but what means are in our power and what actions are the wisest and most helpful.

Malfunctions of Compassion

The feeling of compassion is a common reaction to others' suffering. Even very young children seem to experience it. Yet compassion can malfunction in many ways if it doesn't grow from this feeling into a properly formed emotion and, eventually, into a virtue. We highlight four possible malfunctions that are especially important for public engagement.

First, compassion malfunctions when we restrict it to those who are immediately present to us. Often compassion is about responding to the suffering we encounter firsthand. But the Gospels include multiple stories of Jesus acting compassionately by healing people who were far away from him (Luke 7:1–10; John 4:46–53). Instantaneous communication and highly developed global networks mean that we both regularly encounter the suffering of very distant people and have some ability to address it. We cannot claim ignorance or impotence. Not to respond with compassion is simply callous and unloving.

Second, we might make mistaken judgments about how serious suffering should be in order to motivate compassion. Inspired by Aristotle's (384–322 BC) famous discussion of pity, Martha Nussbaum argues that to feel compassion toward someone implies that we think that person's suffering meets a certain standard of seriousness.[4] There are two mistakes we could make when determining where to put the threshold of seriousness. We could put it too low or too high. If we put it too low, both the agents and the recipients of compassion will be annoyed. If we put the threshold too high, however, we will trivialize serious suffering, treat the needy heartlessly, and fail to respond to their grave situations. While both of these are distortions of compassion, trivializing others' suffering is likely more common and the more harmful of the two.

Third, it would be a mistake to think, like Aristotle for instance, that we should have compassion only for those who do not deserve their suffering.[5] Perhaps this is an intuitive idea. Why should it

bother me when others suffer their just deserts? Yet compassion for
those who suffer as the result of their own failings and misdeeds is
central to the Christian faith. Consider the story of the prodigal
son (Luke 15:11–32). By just about any measure, the son brought
his suffering upon himself. He asked to have his inheritance early,
and he squandered his fortune. And yet when he returned in shame
to his father's house, "while he was still far off, his father saw him
and was filled with compassion" (v. 20). The question of whether
the son deserved suffering doesn't even come up. In case you're
tempted to object that the father in the story represents God, and
thus giving compassion to the unworthy applies only to God, recall
that earlier in the same Gospel Jesus commanded his followers to
"be merciful, just as your Father is merciful" (6:36).

Finally, compassion malfunctions when it is restricted only to
individuals. Our paragons of compassion are generally people who
are moved to act by the suffering of one person they encounter—
say, an orphan on the street or a cancer patient in need of a kidney
transplant. The example of Jesus, however, shows that compassion should not be directed exclusively to individuals. Consider
this passage from Matthew: "When he saw the crowds, he had
compassion for them, because they were harassed and helpless,
like sheep without a shepherd" (Matt. 9:35–36). We saw earlier
that Jesus had compassion for an individual widow. Here Jesus
observes something about the crowds that stokes his compassion.
Indeed, by comparing the crowd to a flock of sheep, Jesus suggests
that there's something about them *as a group* that brings out his
compassion—namely, the fact that they aren't much of a group.
They *should* be a well-tended flock, but instead they're aimless
and disorganized. Shaped by our commitment to Christ, we too
ought to have compassion for those who suffer in and as groups.

The virtue of compassion requires a great deal of wisdom. For
example, saying that compassion shouldn't be limited to people
who are nearby or to individuals alone leaves a host of questions
unanswered. Which nearby or distant suffering people should I

assist with my obviously limited resources? The ones suffering most severely, the ones I'm most confident I could actually help, or someone else? What kind of help should I provide? Should I do what those who suffer ask me to, what I think will be most helpful, or something else? And so on.

There are no easy answers to these questions. We have to greet each situation as it comes and, relying on the guidance of the Spirit, do our best to discern what we should do. We can say, however, that Christian compassion cannot exclude those who suffer as a group, who are far from us, or who supposedly "had it coming," and it must not blithely dismiss others' claims that they are suffering seriously.

To get a sense for what this dynamic, expansive compassion looks like, consider the antitrafficking organization Love146 and its cofounder Rob Morris. When Morris tells the story of how Love146 got started, compassion is right at the heart of it. Being struck by compassion for particular trafficked children transformed Morris's abstract commitment to the antitrafficking cause into spirited commitment to concrete people and ignited Love146's multifaceted work, which runs from survivor care to fund-raising communications to legislative activism. Counterintuitively, Morris thinks compassion—which he describes, using a phrase from Henri Nouwen (1932–96) and his cowriters, as "full immersion in the condition of being human"—is key to avoiding the burnout and cynicism that threaten every activist.[6] The moment the horridness you encounter doesn't hit you in the gut, Morris thinks, is the moment you begin both to lose the driving force of action and to forfeit something of your own humanity. So rather than developing thick skin to cope with the awful realities he encounters in his work, Morris works to keep his skin thin. As an organization, Love146 seeks to be compassionate in all its work. It also acknowledges the possibility of distorting compassion, especially in his organization's case by portraying the people it works with as *merely* sufferers rather than complex human beings. Such conscientious compassion is vital to faithful public discipleship.[7]

Resources for Further Reflection

Introductory Reading

Austin, Michael W. "Compassion." In *Being Good: Christian Virtues for Everyday Life*, edited by Michael W. Austin and R. Douglas Geivett, 185–203. Grand Rapids: Eerdmans, 2012. Austin analyzes the cognitive, affective, and active elements of compassion and includes suggestions on how to develop it.

Bergant, Dianne. "Compassion in the Bible." In *Compassionate Ministry*, edited by Gary Sapp, 9–34. Birmingham, AL: Religious Education, 1993. This study of the vision of compassion in the Christian Scriptures argues that biblical compassion has roots in both intimate familial love and divine love and must be extended universally, even to those whose suffering is deserved.

Bloom, Paul. "Against Empathy." *Boston Review*, September 10, 2014. http://bostonreview.net/forum/paul-bloom-against -empathy. The psychologist Paul Bloom argues for the moral significance of reflective compassion over feelings of empathy, and a number of philosophers, psychologists, and theologians respond.

McNeill, Donald P., Douglas A. Morrison, and Henri J. M. Nouwen. *Compassion: A Reflection on the Christian Life*. Garden City, NY: Doubleday, 1982. This book offers a profound reflection on the compassion of Christ and how it can and should replace the competitiveness at the center of our lives.

Palmer, Jack. "Warning: No Compassion. Proceed with Caution." *God's Politics*, October 5, 2011. http://sojo.net/blogs/2011/10/05 /warning-no-compassion-proceed-caution. Palmer argues that compassion is precisely what is lacking in contemporary politics and economics.

Advanced Study

Farley, Margaret A. *Compassionate Respect: A Feminist Approach to Medical Ethics and Other Questions.* New York: Paulist Press, 2002. Through an engagement with issues of medical ethics and global health crises, Farley shows that true compassion requires respect and true respect requires compassion, thus linking the topics of the last two chapters.

Nussbaum, Martha. "Compassion: The Basic Social Emotion." *Social Philosophy and Policy* 13 (1996): 27–58. Nussbaum's essay is an excellent defense of the importance of compassion in public life through a deep engagement with the Western philosophical tradition. See also the more developed argument in her *Upheavals of Thought: The Intelligence of Emotions* (Cambridge: Cambridge University Press, 2001).

O'Connell, Maureen. *Compassion: Loving Our Neighbor in an Age of Globalization.* Maryknoll, NY: Orbis, 2009. This impassioned and insightful book responds to the "urgent premise" that given the dehumanizing suffering in our world, Christians must embrace compassion as the definitive characteristic of our discipleship.

Wolterstorff, Nicholas. "Augustine's Break with Eudaimonism." In *Justice: Rights and Wrongs*, 180–206. Princeton: Princeton University Press, 2008. Wolterstorff argues that Augustine's engagement with the Christian Scriptures, and particularly with their affirmation of compassion, led him to break with the dominant approach to ethics in the ancient world.

AFTERWORD

In the introduction we said that this book is an invitation to conversation and to action. We meant it. Our communities need vibrant conversation to thrive. The church flourishes as a community when followers of Christ deliberate with one another about the implications of our common faith. Civic communities flourish when their members debate public questions in good faith and in pursuit of common goods. Such conversation is all too rare today. Let's exemplify it.

Our communities also need action—courageous, humble, just, respectful, compassionate engagement aimed at genuine flourishing. We can't just all go about our business and expect the issues of our common life together to work themselves out. They demand careful attention and thoughtful action. Let's rise to the challenge.

Through the Spirit, Christ is at work in the whole world, pulling and pushing and nudging and luring it into resemblance with the coming kingdom. Our own flourishing, no less than the flourishing of our ecclesial and civic communities, lies in responding to this call, aligning our lives with Christ's, and participating in his work in the world. Let's seek to discern that work and join in it together.

ACKNOWLEDGMENTS

We would be remiss not to begin by thanking Robert Hosack at Baker, whose interest in publishing an elaboration of Miroslav's 2012 Facebook posts got the ball rolling on this project. Both he and the entire staff at Baker have been a pleasure to work with.

In the course of writing, we've benefited immensely from the input of two remarkable student colleagues. Toni Alimi came on board when we were up against deadlines and provided not only research help (compiling and annotating the lists of resources for further reflection in chaps. 10 and 15) but sharp observations and spirited critiques as well. Princeton is lucky to have him as a doctoral student. No one has influenced the course of our writing more than Ryan Darr, a doctoral student in religious ethics at Yale. Ryan compiled and annotated the great majority of the lists of resources for further reflection (all except chaps. 1–3, 10, and 15). He joined our weekly meetings from nearly the beginning and never failed to move the conversation in constructive directions. He posed questions we never would have thought to ask, formulated many of our thoughts better than we could, and argued cogently when he thought we were on the wrong course. Over the course of writing, our thinking has often bent in the direction of his, and where it hasn't, his astute criticism and apt articulation of alternative views have prompted us to sharpen our arguments and clarify their presentation. It won't be surprising if someday in the not-too-distant future he writes a book that makes this one outdated.

From Miroslav: I am grateful to the staff at the Yale Center for Faith and Culture for keeping me undisturbed in my "writing den" and suffering patiently my late responses to emails or forgotten assignments. I have benefited immensely from their vision, dedication, competence, and hard work. Yale University and the dean of its divinity school, Gregory E. Sterling, have been once more generous in providing me with a research leave during which I worked on this book. I have tried to keep my sons and my work from bumping into each other, but I am grateful for their indulgence when, though spending time with them, I wandered into my own world; Aaron in particular felt more of my stress than he should have, including my bailing out on occasion from our afternoon one-on-one soccer matches. I have incurred many debts to Jessica, my wife, while writing this book. In the chapter on debt, Ryan and I argued that one should never borrow more than one can repay, and yet that's what I have done with her. She has been a generous and unwavering supporter.

From Ryan: Two communities have been my intellectual and spiritual homes for more than five years now: the Yale theology program and the Elm City Vineyard church (ECV). Thank you to all who are or have been a part of them. A few in particular ought to be singled out: Janna Gonwa and LaQruishia Gill helped clarify my thinking on punishment one evening on the New Jersey Turnpike. Alysia Harris provided characteristically incisive and challenging comments on the chapter on policing. Josh Williams has led ECV into thoughtful and faithful public engagement in our New Haven community and inspired me to think more deeply and follow Jesus a bit more courageously in many of the areas discussed in the book. Weekly lunches with Matt Croasmun, Ryan Darr, and Todd Kennedy have done as much as anything else to shape my thought over the last few years.

Ever true to form, my dad, Paul Linz, was up for spirited, guile-less conversations at every opportunity and was a bottomless well of encouragement. Conversations with him and with my father-in-law, Ross Jutsum, always helped me wield off despair over the possibility of constructive Christian conversations about political disagreements. My mom, Linda McAnnally, did her best to instill in me an ethos of care for the common good and attentiveness to the margins. She's also my go-to sociologist for data on all things criminological. My wife, Heidi, patiently fielded stylistic ques-tions, indulged my over-complicating worries, and maintained a matter-of-fact faith that I was up for this task, all the while being an exemplar of faithful public engagement in her own work. Heidi and I are both immensely grateful to the wonderful group of child-care workers from New Haven to Nairobi, Marta Jiménez chief among them, who have generously loved and attended to our daughter, Grace, as my work hours have expanded. And last, a thank-you that will not be understood for some years yet, to my little Grace herself—a joyous parable for me of God's ever-greater grace, who has been learning well what it means to love and be loved by someone who doesn't have it all sorted out.

We have dedicated this book to Jürgen Moltmann. Moltmann is family—*academic* family: he was Miroslav's *Doktorvater* and is therefore Ryan's "grand-*Doktorvater*." Like no other theologian of his generation, he has produced theology, epitomized perhaps best in his *The Crucified God* (1972), that is both existential and academic, pastoral and political, innovative and traditional, read-able and demanding, contextual and universal—and all of this in explicating the bearing of central Christian themes, such as the crucifixion and resurrection of Jesus Christ or the trinitarian life of God, on fundamental human experiences. For both of us, he is the exemplary contemporary public theologian.

NOTES

Introduction

1. For an extension of this argument to other world religions, see Miroslav Volf, *Flourishing: Why We Need Religion in a Globalized World* (New Haven: Yale University Press, 2016). For a discussion of the contribution that *A Public Faith: How Followers of Christ Should Serve the Common Good* (Grand Rapids: Brazos, 2011) makes to reflection on the place and role of the Christian faith in pluralistic societies, see *Political Theology* 14, no. 6 (2013), a special issue on the book, with contributions from Nicholas Wolterstorff, John G. Stackhouse, Jayne Svenungsson, M. T. Dávila, Julie Hanlon Rubio, Lenn E. Goodman, David Fergusson, and Yasir Qadhi, as well as a response by Miroslav.

2. On public theology, see Michael Welker, *God the Revealed: Christology*, trans. Douglas W. Stott (Grand Rapids: Eerdmans, 2013), 244–47. See also Wolfgang Huber, *Gerechtigkeit und Recht: Grundlinien christlicher Rechtslehre* (Gütersloh: Gütersloher Verlag, 2006), 12–13.

3. See Williams's profound reflections on language in *The Edge of Words: God and the Habits of Language* (London: Bloomsbury, 2014), especially chap. 3.

Chapter 1: Christ the Center and Norm

1. Jürgen Moltmann, *The Crucified God: The Cross of Christ as the Foundation and Criticism of Christian Theology*, trans. R. A. Wilson and John Bowden (Minneapolis: Fortress, 1993), 126–45.

2. See Michael Welker, *God the Revealed: Christology*, trans. Douglas W. Stott (Grand Rapids: Eerdmans, 2013), 192–97, 261.

3. Our point that the hope for a kingdom in which God will be all in all ought to inform our public engagement stands independently of whether we think that this verse implies universal salvation or not.

4. Karl Barth, "The Christian Community and the Civil Community," in *Community, Church, and State: Three Essays* (Eugene, OR: Wipf & Stock, 2004), 149–89.

Chapter 2: Christ, the Spirit, and Flourishing

1. On the contrast between political religions and politically engaged religions, see Miroslav Volf, *Flourishing: Why We Need Religion in a Globalized World* (New Haven: Yale University Press, 2016), 84–87. On Christ as the end of political religion, see Giorgio Agamben, *Pilate and Jesus*, trans. Adam Kotsko (Stanford, CA: Stanford University Press, 2015), especially 55–57.

2. Martin Luther, *The Freedom of a Christian*, in *Martin Luther: Selections from His Writings*, ed. John Dillenberger (New York: Anchor, 1962), 75–76.

3. Heribert Mühlen originally suggested this idea in *Una Mystica Persona: Die Kirche als das Mysterium der Heilsgeschichtlichen Identität des Heiligen Geistes in Christus und den Christen; Eine Person in vielen Personen* (Paderborn: Ferdinand Schöning, 1968).

4. For a more extended discussion of this subject, see Miroslav Volf and Maurice Lee, "The Spirit and the Church," in *Advents of the Spirit: An Introduction to the Current Study of Pneumatology*, ed. Bradford E. Hinze and D. Lyle Dabney (Milwaukee: Marquette University Press, 2001), 380–407.

5. See Miroslav Volf, *Work in the Spirit: Toward a Theology of Work* (New York: Oxford University Press, 1991), the main thesis of which is that all work of Christians ought to be seen and practiced as "work in the Spirit."

6. Nicholas Wolterstorff makes the distinction between leading life well and life going well in *Justice: Rights and Wrongs* (Princeton: Princeton University Press, 2008), 145–47. We think a complete account of human flourishing needs the third facet.

7. That is to say not that we can fully live life well without God's grace but rather that grace fulfills our agency rather than destroying it. "For freedom Christ has set us free" (Gal. 5:1).

8. Claus Westermann, "Peace [*Shalom*] in the Old Testament," in *The Meaning of Peace: Biblical Studies*, ed. Perry B. Yoder and Willard M. Swartley, trans. Walter W. Sawatsky (Elkhart, IN: Institute of Mennonite Studies, 2001), 44.

9. On this point, see Agamben, *Pilate and Jesus*, 26–38.

Chapter 3: Reading in Contexts

1. Obviously, this is not the only way of reading these texts that keeps them from justifying the slaughter of one's enemies. Many Jewish interpretations do the same without appeal to Jesus.

2. Martin Luther King Jr., *Strength to Love* (Philadelphia: Fortress, 1981), 22.

3. Ibid., 56.

4. Martin Luther King Jr., *Why We Can't Wait* (New York: Signet Classics, 2000), 50–51.

Chapter 4: Wealth

1. *The Sayings of the Desert Fathers: The Alphabetical Collection*, trans. Benedicta Ward, SLG, rev. ed. (Kalamazoo, MI: Cistercian Publications, 1984), 8.

2. See Miroslav Volf, *Work in the Spirit: Toward a Theology of Work* (New York: Oxford University Press, 1991).

3. Book of Common Prayer, "A Collect for Peace" (Morning Prayer Rite II).

4. See Michael J. Sandel, *What Money Can't Buy: The Moral Limits of Markets* (New York: Farrar, Straus & Giroux, 2012), 16–62.

Chapter 5: The Environment

1. "Facts about Rainforests," The Nature Conservancy, accessed June 5, 2015, http://www.nature.org/ourinitiatives/urgentissues/rainforests/rainforests-facts.xml; Howard Falcon-Lang, "Anthropocene: Have Humans Created a New Geological Age?," *BBC News*, May 11, 2011, http://www.bbc.com/news/science-environment-13335683. On climate change, see Intergovernmental Panel on Climate Change, "Summary for Policymakers," in *Climate Change 2014: Synthesis Report. Contribution of Working Groups I, II and III to the Fifth Assessment Report of the Intergovernmental Panel on Climate Change* (Geneva: IPCC, 2014), http://www.ipcc.ch/pdf/assessment-report /ar5/syr/AR5_SYR_FINAL_SPM.pdf.

2. Jürgen Moltmann, *Creating a Just Future*, trans. John Bowden (Philadelphia: Trinity Press International, 1989), 68.

3. Moltmann often speaks of this distinction between owning/disposing of the earth and "using" it. See, for example, ibid., 56.

4. It's practically impossible to get a good estimate of the number of extinctions currently occurring because we don't know how many species there are. It could be that we'll never even know of the existence of the vast majority of species that go extinct because of human activity. See "How Many Species Are We Losing?," World Wildlife Fund, accessed June 5, 2015, http://wwf.panda.org/about_our_earth /biodiversity/biodiversity/.

5. See Tim Jackson, *Prosperity without Growth* (London: Earthscan, 2009), for a challenging presentation of the idea that we can, and must, learn to thrive without any more economic growth.

6. The figure is for purchasing power parity GDP in 2014 US dollars. See "World," *The World Factbook* (Washington, DC: Central Intelligence Agency, 2013), https:// www.cia.gov/library/publications/resources/the-world-factbook/geos/xx.html.

7. "Poverty Overview," The World Bank, accessed June 3, 2015, http://www.world bank.org/en/topic/poverty/overview.

8. Stephen M. Meyer, "The Economic Impact of Environmental Regulation," *Journal of Environmental Law and Practice* 3 (1995): 4–15, http://web.mit.edu/polisci /mpepp/Reports/Econ%20Impact%20Enviro%20Reg.pdf. Additionally, in 2013 the White House Office of Management and Budget estimated that while between 2002 and 2012 EPA regulations had an economic cost of $30.4–$36.5 billion, such regulations also led to benefits of $112–$637 billion ("2013 Draft Report to Congress on the Benefit and Costs of Federal Regulations and Agency Compliance with the Unfunded Mandates Reform Act," https://www.whitehouse.gov/sites/default/files /omb/inforeg/2013_cb/draft_2013_cost_benefit_report.pdf).

Chapter 6: Education

1. Barack Obama, "What's Possible for Our Children," text published by the *Denver Post*, May 28, 2008, http://www.denverpost.com/ci_9405199.

2. Governor Walker claims not to have known about the proposed changes before they were publicized.

3. John Henry Newman, *The Idea of a University* (Assumption, IL: Assumption Press, 2014), 90 (1.5.6).

4. See Anthony T. Kronman, *Education's End: Why Our Colleges and Universities Have Given Up on the Meaning of Life* (New Haven: Yale University Press, 2008).

5. See Miroslav Volf, "Hunger for Infinity: Christian Faith and the Dynamics of Economic Progress," in *Captive to the Word of God: Engaging the Scriptures for Contemporary Theological Reflection* (Grand Rapids: Eerdmans, 2010), 161–64.

6. The same is true of pluralistic universities. See Miroslav Volf, "Life Worth Living: Christian Faith and the Crisis of the Universities," *ABC Religion and Ethics*, April 30, 2014, http://www.abc.net.au/religion/articles/2014/04/30/3994889.htm.

7. See, for example, Rachel Glennerster, Michael Kremer, Isaac Mbiti, and Kudzai Takavarasha, "Access and Quality in the Kenyan Education System," May 2011, http://www.povertyactionlab.org/publication/access-and-quality-kenyan-education -system, 5, 15; Anna T. Schurmann, "Review of the Bangladesh Female Secondary School Stipend Project Using a Social Exclusion Framework," *Journal of Health, Population, and Nutrition* 27 (2009): 505–17.

8. College Board, "Average Rates of Growth of Published Charges by Decade," accessed June 3, 2015, http://trends.collegeboard.org/college-pricing/figures-tables /average-rates-growth-published-charges-decade.

Chapter 7: Work and Rest

1. This is a rough definition. Miroslav works to provide a more precise one in *Work in the Spirit: Toward a Theology of Work* (New York: Oxford University Press, 1991).

2. Jürgen Moltmann, *Ethics of Hope* (Minneapolis: Fortress, 2012), 233.

3. According to the Bureau of Labor Statistics, in 2012 the median annual pay for maids and housekeeping cleaners was $19,570. For food and beverage service workers, it was $18,400. Bureau of Labor Statistics, US Department of Labor, *Occupational Outlook Handbook, 2014–15 Edition*, Maids and Housekeeping Cleaners, http:// www.bls.gov/ooh/building-and-grounds-cleaning/maids-and-housekeeping-cleaners .htm; Food and Beverage Serving and Related Workers, http://www.bls.gov/ooh/food -preparation-and-serving/food-and-beverage-serving-and-related-workers.htm.

4. Lydia Saad, "The '40-Hour' Work Week Is Actually Longer—by Seven Hours," Gallup, August 29, 2014, http://www.gallup.com/poll/175286/hour-workweek-actually -longer-seven-hours.aspx; Rebecca Ray, Milla Sanes, and John Schmitt, "No-Vacation Nation Revisited" (Washington, DC: Center for Economic and Policy Research, 2013); Bureau of Labor Statistics, "Employee Benefits in the United States—March 2014," US Department of Labor Press Release USDL-14-1348, July 25, 2014, http://www .bls.gov/ncs/ebs/sp/ebnr0020.pdf.

Chapter 8: Poverty

1. "Hunger Statistics," World Food Programme, accessed June 3, 2015, http://www.wfp.org/hunger/stats; "Child Hunger," United Nations, accessed June 3, 2015, http://www.un.org/en/globalissues/briefingpapers/food/childhunger.shtml; "Hunger and Poverty Fact Sheet," Feeding America, accessed June 3, 2015, http://www.feeding america.org/hunger-in-america/impact-of-hunger/hunger-and-poverty/hunger-and -poverty-fact-sheet.html.

2. A very small sampling: Isa. 3:14–15; 10:1–4; Ezek. 16:49; 22:29–31; Amos 2:4–7; Zech. 7:8–10.

3. Pope Benedict XVI (Joseph Ratzinger), *Jesus of Nazareth: The Infancy Narratives*, trans. Philip J. Whitmore (New York: Image, 2012), 72.

4. John Chrysostom, "Second Sermon on Lazarus and the Rich Man," in *On Wealth and Poverty*, trans. Catharine P. Roth (Crestwood, NY: St. Vladimir's Seminary Press, 1984), 50.

5. Basil the Great, "I Will Pull Down My Barns," in Peter C. Phan, *Social Thought: Message of the Fathers of the Church* (Wilmington, DE: Michael Glazier, 1984), 117.

6. "Poverty Overview," World Bank, accessed June 3, 2015, http://www.worldbank .org/en/topic/poverty/overview.

7. Computed using wealth estimates for the bottom three deciles of global adult population found in Credit Suisse's *Global Wealth Databook 2015* (Anthony Shorrocks, James B. Davies, and Rodrigo Lluberas [Zurich: Credit Suisse, 2015], 23–26, 110), along with their population estimates (approximately 4.772 billion adults worldwide). The asset-poor tend disproportionately to be women (see Carmen Diana Deere and Cheryl R. Doss, "The Gender Asset Gap: What Do We Know and Why Does It Matter?," *Feminist Economics* 12 [2006]: 1–50).

8. Shorrocks, Davies, Lluberas, *Global Wealth Databook 2015*, 110. Our thanks to Cheryl Doss for her advice on this paragraph.

9. Adam Smith, *An Inquiry into the Nature and Causes of the Wealth of Nations* 5.2.2.4, ed. Edwin Cannan (New York: Random House, 1994), 938–39.

10. See Miroslav Volf, *Flourishing: Why We Need Religion in a Globalized World* (New Haven: Yale University Press, 2016), 202–5.

11. Calculated by Toni Alimi from the Bureau of Economic Analysis's data for fourth-quarter GDP in 1982 and 2014 (Bureau of Economic Analysis, "Current-Dollar and 'Real' GDP," National Economic Accounts, accessed June 3, 2015, http://www .bea.gov/national/index.htm#gdp).

12. US Census Bureau, "Number in Poverty and Poverty Rate," from *Current Population Survey, 1960 to 2014 Annual Social and Economic Supplements*, accessed June 3, 2015, http://www.census.gov/hhes/www/poverty/data/incpovhlth/2013/figure4.pdf.

13. Chrysostom, "Second Sermon on Lazarus and the Rich Man," 54.

14. Groups such as Innovations for Poverty Action (www.poverty-action.org) are starting to provide reliable evidence for the efficacy of some programs, but there is still much that we don't know about how to reduce poverty.

Chapter 9: Borrowing and Lending

1. "Consumers Rely on Car Financing More Than Ever," ConsumerReports.org, September 6, 2013, http://www.consumerreports.org/cro/news/2013/09/car-financing -on-rise-loans-and-leases/index.htm.

2. Jesus tells the parable in reply to Peter's question about how many times to forgive another member of the church, but that doesn't mean it is only relevant for "moral" forgiveness. As the two versions of the Lord's Prayer (Matt. 6:9–15 and Luke 11:2–4) illustrate, forgiveness of sins and forgiveness of debts are closely related.

3. Luke Bretherton, "Neither a Borrower nor a Lender Be? Scripture, Usury and the Call for Responsible Lending," *Christian Ethics Today* 21 (2013): 3.

4. "There Are More Payday Lenders in the U.S. Than McDonald's," *NBC News*, November 24, 2014, http://www.nbcnews.com/business/economy/there-are-more -payday-lenders-u-s-mcdonalds-n255156; Consumer Financial Protection Bureau, "Payday Loans and Direct Deposit Advances," White Paper, April 24, 2013, http:// files.consumerfinance.gov/f/201304_cfpb_payday-dap-whitepaper.pdf.

5. Christine LaMontagne, "NerdWallet Health Finds Medical Bankruptcy Accounts for Majority of Personal Bankruptcies," NerdWallet, March 26, 2014, http:// www.nerdwallet.com/blog/health/2014/03/26/medical-bankruptcy/.

Chapter 11: New Life

1. As is probably already evident, both of us are men. In this chapter, we'll make some normative claims with respect to an experience (pregnancy) that we can never know "from the inside." In doing so, we risk participating in a history of reflection on these questions that has fairly consistently ignored or marginalized women's voices. While we hope that our remarks have been shaped by postures of listening to women's voices, we welcome correction and clarification, and we fully expect that some revisions will be in order.

2. See James Mumford, *Ethics at the Beginning of Life: A Phenomenological Critique* (Oxford: Oxford University Press, 2013).

3. "Baby Bonus," Singapore Ministry of Social and Family Development, updated June 15, 2015, http://www.babybonus.msf.gov.sg/parent/; "Maternity Package," Kela, updated February 24, 2015, http://www.kela.fi/web/en/maternitypackage.

4. We are convinced that if accessible and affordable birth control as part of these services reduces abortions, it too should be provided. We acknowledge that the *magisterium* of the Roman Catholic Church disagrees. We think, however, that the Catholic hierarchy's reasoning on this question is mistaken. For a promising direction for Christian (especially Protestant) reflection about birth control, see Kathryn D. Blanchard, "The Gift of Contraception: Calvin, Barth, and a Lost Protestant Conversation," *Journal of the Society of Christian Ethics* 27 (2007): 225–49.

5. See, e.g., *Catechism of the Catholic Church*, 2nd ed., 2270, 2274, http://www .usccb.org/beliefs-and-teachings/what-we-believe/catechism/catechism-of-the-catholic -church/epub/index.cfm#.

6. See David Albert Jones, *The Soul of the Embryo: An Enquiry into the Status of the Human Embryo in the Christian Tradition* (London: Continuum, 2004), 109–24, for an overview of the positions of various premodern Christian thinkers. The view of Thomas Aquinas that abortion even before "ensoulment" is a mortal sin illustrates that the question of when life begins does not necessarily answer the question of the justifiability of abortion by itself. See John Haldane and Patrick Lee, "Aquinas on Human Ensoulment, Abortion and the Value of Life," *Philosophy* 78 (2003): 261–62.

7. "Miscarriage," United States National Library of Medicine, last updated November 8, 2012, http://www.nlm.nih.gov/medlineplus/ency/article/001488.htm.

Chapter 12: Health and Sickness

1. Centers for Medicare and Medicaid Services, "Historical," in *National Health Expenditure Accounts*, modified December 9, 2014, http://www.cms.gov/Research -Statistics-Data-and-Systems/Statistics-Trends-and-Reports/NationalHealthExpend Data/NationalHealthAccountsHistorical.html; Christine LaMontagne, "NerdWallet Health Finds Medical Bankruptcy Accounts for Majority of Personal Bankruptcies," NerdWallet, March 26, 2014, http://www.nerdwallet.com/blog/health/2014/03/26 /medical-bankruptcy/; Tami Luhby, "Millions Can't Afford to Go to the Doctor," *CNN Money*, April 26, 2013, http://money.cnn.com/2013/04/26/news/economy/health -care-cost/; Committee on Population, "Explore Findings from the New Report: 'U.S. Health in International Perspectives,'" The National Academies of Sciences, Engineering, and Medicine, accessed June 3, 2015, http://sites.nationalacademies .org/DBASSE/CPOP/DBASSE_080393#deaths-from-all-causes; Richard Knox, "U.S. Ranks below 16 Other Rich Countries in Health Report," National Public Radio, January 9, 2013, http://www.npr.org/sections/health-shots/2013/01/09/168976602/u-s -ranks-below-16-other-rich-countries-in-health-report.

2. World Health Organization, "Malaria," WHO Fact Sheet no. 94, accessed June 3, 2015, http://www.who.int/mediacentre/factsheets/fs094/en; UNICEF, "Goal: Reduce Child Mortality," Millennium Development Goals, accessed June 3, 2015, http://www.unicef.org/mdg/index_childmortality.htm; World Health Organization, *World Health Statistics 2011* (Geneva: WHO Press, 2011), 124; WHO/UNICEF Joint Monitoring Programme for Water Supply and Sanitation, "Progress on Sanitation and Drinking Water 2010," 2015, http://www.wssinfo.org/documents; cf. "3 Things Most of the World Can't Do," Water.org, accessed January 15, 2016, http://static .water.org.s3.amazonaws.com/public/02_Sanitation.jpeg.

3. "Fact File on Health Inequities," World Health Organization, accessed June 3, 2015, http://www.who.int/sdhconference/background/news/facts/en/.

4. Centers for Disease Control, "CDC Health Disparities and Inequalities Re- port—United States, 2013," *Morbidity and Mortality Weekly Report Supplement* 62, no. 3 (November 2013), http://www.cdc.gov/mmwr/pdf/other/su6203.pdf.

5. "2011 Quick Facts," American Society of Plastic Surgeons, http://www.plastic surgery.org/Documents/news-resources/statistics/2011-statistics/2011_Stats_Quick _Facts.pdf.

6. World Health Organization, "Financing Malaria Control," in *World Malaria Report 2011*, http://www.who.int/malaria/world_malaria_report_2011/WMR2011 _chapter3.pdf.

7. See Environmental Protection Agency, "Contaminated Lands," in *America's Children and the Environment*, 3rd ed., EPA 240-R-13-001, 95–104, http://www.epa .gov/ace/pdfs/ACE3_2013.pdf.

8. "Food Deserts," US Department of Agriculture, accessed June 3, 2015, http:// apps.ams.usda.gov/fooddeserts/fooddeserts.aspx.

9. Karl Barth laid out a general principle along these lines: "The general liv- ing conditions of all, or at least of as many as possible, are to be shaped in such a way that they make not just a negative but a positive preventative contribution to their health, as is the case already in varying degrees with the privileged" (*Church Dogmatics* III/4, ed. Geoffrey Bromiley and Thomas Forsyth Torrance [Edinburgh: T&T Clark, 1961], 363).

10. For a thought-provoking discussion of how commodification affects a variety of goods today, see Michael J. Sandel, *What Money Can't Buy: The Moral Limits of Markets* (New York: Farrar, Straus & Giroux, 2012).

11. Paul Farmer, *Pathologies of Power: Health, Human Rights, and the New War on the Poor* (Berkeley: University of California Press, 2005), 152.

12. "Free Distribution or Cost-Sharing: Evidence from a Malaria Prevention Experiment in Kenya," Innovations for Poverty Action, accessed June 3, 2015, http://www.poverty-action.org/project/bednets.

Chapter 13: Aging Life

1. Friedrich Nietzsche, *The Gay Science*, ed. Bernard Williams (Cambridge: Cambridge University Press, 2001), §3; "'Improving' Humanity," in *The Anti-Christ, Ecce Homo, Twilight of the Idols, and Other Writings*, ed. Aaron Ridley and Judith Norman (Cambridge: Cambridge University Press, 2005), §5.

2. William Shakespeare, *As You Like It*, act 2, scene 7.

3. Drew DeSilver, "Who's Poor in America? 50 Years into the 'War on Poverty,' a Data Portrait," Pew Research Center, January 13, 2014, http://www.pewresearch.org/fact-tank/2014/01/13/whos-poor-in-america-50-years-into-the-war-on-poverty-a-data-portrait/.

Chapter 14: Ending Life

1. Nearly half of Americans die in a hospital. "Facing Death: Facts and Figures," PBS *Frontline*, November 23, 2010, http://www.pbs.org/wgbh/pages/frontline/facing-death/facts-and-figures/.

2. Loulla-Mae Eleftheriou-Smith, "Brittany Maynard: Terminally Ill Euthanasia Campaigner Dying of Cancer Ends Her Life by Assisted Suicide," *Independent*, November 3, 2014, http://www.independent.co.uk/news/people/brittany-maynard-dead-terminally-ill-cancer-patient-ends-life-by-assisted-suicide-9834808.html.

3. Penelope Wang, "Cutting the High Cost of End-of-Life Care," *Time.com*, December 12, 2012, http://time.com/money/2793643/cutting-the-high-cost-of-end-of-life-care/.

4. Other accounts of the special preciousness of human life might start from the exceptional status given humans as bearers of the image of God or from the fact that God chose to assume human being in the life of Jesus, thus sanctifying all humanity. Whichever of these routes one takes, it is sure to lead to the conclusion that intentionally killing a human being is an evil.

5. Jürgen Moltmann, "Expectation" (unpublished manuscript, June 2015), 7.

6. "65+ in the United States: 2010," US Census Bureau, P23–212 (Washington, DC: US Government Printing Office, 2014), https://www.census.gov/content/dam/Census/library/publications/2014/demo/p23-212.pdf, 5.

7. Euthanasia can also apply to nonhuman animals and is a commonly accepted veterinary practice.

8. PAS could in principle involve means of death other than the use of lethal drugs, but we are not aware of any proposals that such other forms of PAS should be legalized.

9. Gilbert Meilaender, "Euthanasia and Christian Vision," *Thought* 57 (1982): 472.

10. This argument assumes that there is a moral distinction between killing someone and letting someone die. Moral philosophers such as James Rachels have argued

that there is no such distinction (see Rachels, "Active and Passive Euthanasia," in *Applied Ethics*, ed. Peter Singer [Oxford: Oxford University Press, 1986], 29–35). Meilaender offers a version of likely the most common Christian argument in favor of the distinction between killing and letting die when he claims that our assessment of the results and motives of an act ought to be shaped by its *aim*. In some but not all cases, killing and letting die have different aims and so are morally different (see Meilaender, "Euthanasia and Christian Vision," 465–75).

11. Karl Barth reminds us that "life is no second God, and therefore the respect due to it cannot rival the reverence owed to God" (*Church Dogmatics* III/4, ed. Geoffrey Bromiley and Thomas Forsyth Torrance [Edinburgh: T&T Clark, 1961], 342).

12. Meilaender, "Euthanasia and Christian Vision," 473.

13. By "terminal illness" we mean a condition that is both incurable (or at least extremely unlikely to be cured) and lethal.

14. See Rachel Aviv, "The Death Treatment: When Should People with a Nonterminal Illness Be Helped to Die?," *New Yorker*, June 22, 2015, http://www.new yorker.com/magazine/2015/06/22/the-death-treatment.

Chapter 15: Migration

1. Paul Adams, "Migration: Are More People on the Move Than Ever Before?," *BBC News*, May 28, 2015, http://www.bbc.com/news/world-32912867; Somini Sengupta, "60 Million People Fleeing Chaotic Lands, U.N. Says," *New York Times*, June 18, 2015, http://nyti.ms/1GtYhrH.

2. Although each of us has had different experiences leaving a home country and living elsewhere (Miroslav from Croatia to Germany and the United States, and Ryan from the United States to the United Kingdom and Latin America), we're writing as residents of the country with the most immigrants, so we'll focus our remarks on what faithful political engagement with migration would look like in that sort of country.

3. See Miroslav Volf, *Exclusion and Embrace: A Theological Exploration of Identity, Otherness, and Reconciliation* (Nashville: Abingdon, 1996), 50–52, 58–71. See also Volf, *A Public Faith: How Followers of Christ Should Serve the Common Good* (Grand Rapids: Brazos, 2011), 77–97. For the idea of "soft difference," see Volf, "Soft Difference: Church and Culture in 1 Peter," in *Captive to the Word of God: Engaging the Scriptures for Contemporary Theological Reflection* (Grand Rapids: Eerdmans, 2010), 65–90.

4. For more details and reflection on this story, see Luke Bretherton, *Christianity and Contemporary Politics* (Malden, MA: Wiley-Blackwell, 2010), 152–58; and Hillary Cunningham, *God and Caesar at the Rio Grande: Sanctuary and the Politics of Religion* (Minneapolis: University of Minnesota Press, 1995).

5. If the story of the Tower of Babel leads you to worry that linguistic and cultural diversity might be a punishment from God and not a created good, read Walter Brueggemann, *Genesis*, Interpretation: A Bible Commentary for Teaching and Preaching (Louisville: Westminster John Knox, 1982), 97–104.

6. See also Isa. 19:18–25; 60:1–14; Mic. 4:1–4; Rev. 21:24.

7. See "Latest Global Figures," Missing Migrants Project, http://missingmigrants .iom.int/en/latest-global-figures for up-to-date numbers.

8. Tim Padgett, "People Smugglers Inc." *Time*, August 12, 2003, http://content .time.com/time/magazine/article/0,9171,474582-1,00.html.

9. David Iglesias, "Perspectives on Immigration," *Wheaton*, Spring 2015, 23.

Chapter 16: Policing

1. Walter Brueggemann, *Disruptive Grace: Reflections on God, Scripture, and the Church*, ed. Carolyn J. Sharp (Minneapolis: Fortress, 2011), 53.

2. Martin Luther King Jr., "Letter from Birmingham City Jail," in *A Testament of Hope: The Essential Writings of Martin Luther King, Jr.*, ed. James Melvin Washington (New York: Harper & Row, 1986), 295.

3. We echo here John Howard Yoder's phrase "with the grain of the universe," from his discussion of Leo Tolstoy, Mohandas Gandhi, and Martin Luther King Jr. ("The Political Meaning of *Hope*," in *The War of the Lamb: The Ethics of Nonviolence and Peacemaking*, ed. Glen Stassen, Mark Thiessen Nation, and Matt Hamsher [Grand Rapids: Brazos, 2009], 62).

4. Including the different Gospels' versions of the same story, Jesus tells somebody not to be afraid a total of *eighteen* times in the four Gospels.

5. See the astute observations of Jamelle Bouie and Ta-Nehisi Coates about the consequences of letting police officers' fear justify the use of lethal force: Bouie, "Lethal Force as First Resort," *Slate*, December 28, 2015, http://www.slate.com/articles /news_and_politics/politics/2015/12/the_tamir_rice_grand_jury_decision_shows _that_we_give_police_too_wide_a.html; Coates, "The Paranoid Style of American Policing," *The Atlantic*, December 30, 2015, http://www.theatlantic.com/politics /archive/2015/12/illegitimacy-and-american-policing/422094/.

6. For information on implicit bias, see the resources from the Kirwan Institute for the Study of Race and Ethnicity at Ohio State University (http://kirwaninstitute .osu.edu/research/understanding-implicit-bias/).

7. "Black Boys Viewed as Older, Less Innocent Than Whites, Research Finds," American Psychological Association, March 6, 2014, http://www.apa.org/news/press /releases/2014/03/black-boys-older.aspx.

8. This point also implies that in a democratic society the political majority must accept that it is responsible when the police are systematically abusive. See Ta-Nehisi Coates, "Blue Lives Matter," *Atlantic*, December 22, 2014, http://www.theatlantic.com /politics/archive/2014/12/blue-lives-matter-nypd-shooting/383977/.

9. See "Law Enforcement Officers Killed and Assaulted, 2014: Officers Feloniously Killed," US Department of Justice—Federal Bureau of Investigation, https://www .fbi.gov/about-us/cjis/ucr/leoka/2014/officers-feloniously-killed/officers-feloniously -killed.pdf. The comparison with other occupations uses data from the Bureau of Labor Statistics, *Census of Fatal Occupational Injuries, 2014*, specifically the tables "Fatal Occupational Injuries Resulting from Transportation Incidents and Homicides by Occupation, All United States, 2014," http://www.bls.gov/iif/oshwc/cfoi/cftb 0291.pdf, and "Fatal Occupational Injuries, Total Hours Worked, and Rates of Fatal Occupational Injuries by Selected Worker Characteristics, Occupations, and Industries, Civilian Workers, 2014," http://www.bls.gov/iif/oshwc/cfoi/cfoi_rates_2014 hb.pdf.

10. "The Counted: People Killed by Police in the US," *Guardian*, http://www .theguardian.com/us-news/ng-interactive/2015/jun/01/the-counted-police-killings-us -database. Data on police shootings in the United States have been horribly unreliable, in great part because departments are not required to report them and there is no standardized approach to cataloging police use of force.

11. It should be clear that we are using "killed" here to imply the use of nonaccidental violent force and thus not to include negligent manslaughter. Because these numbers are so shocking, it's important for us to show our work. *The Guardian* recorded 178 Black men 18 to 34 years old killed by police in 2015. The US Census Bureau estimates that there were 5,536,665 Black men 18 to 34 years old in the United States in July 2014 (calculated using their figures for 18-to-24-year-olds plus 25-to-29- and 30-to-34-year-olds). Using the same population growth rate for that demographic between 2013 and 2014, we projected 5,613,060 for July 2015. Dividing 179 by 5,613,060 yields the rate of 3.19 per 100,000. Homicide data for 2015 were not yet available at the time of writing, so we used the FBI's 2014 data (4,866 White victims of murder age 18 and over) and the Census Bureau's 2014 estimates (193,000,553 White Americans age 18 and over). Dividing 4,866 by 193,000,553 yields the rate of 2.52 per 100,000. The FBI does not record the race of the victims of justifiable homicides, but even if all the 2014 victims had been White (which they were not), the rate would only rise to 2.89 per 100,000, leaving the comparative point intact. For reference, the incidence of White men 18 to 34 years old killed by police in 2015, calculated using the same method as above for Black men, was 0.98 per 100,000—less than one-third the rate for Black men of the same age. A caveat about our data: we were unable to include people who reported two or more races to the Census Bureau. See "Annual Estimates of the Resident Population by Sex, Age, Race, and Hispanic Origin for the United States and States: April 1, 2010 to July 1, 2014," US Census Bureau, Population Division, http://www.census.gov/popest/data/national/asrh/2014/index.html; "Crime in the United States, 2014: Expanded Homicide Data, Table 2," US Department of Justice—Federal Bureau of Investigation, https://www.fbi.gov/about-us/cjis/ucr/crime-in-the-u.s/2014/crime-in-the-u.s.-2014/tables/expanded-homicide-data/expanded_homicide_data_table_2_murder_victims_by_age_sex_and_race_2014.xls.

12. See "Investigation of the Ferguson Police Department," US Department of Justice, Civil Rights Division, March 4, 2015, http://www.justice.gov/sites/default/files/opa/press-releases/attachments/2015/03/04/ferguson_police_department_report.pdf, which shows that American police are not immune to grave abuses of power and flagrant disregard for the law.

13. See Sue Rahr, "From Warriors to Guardians—Returning American Police Culture to Democratic Ideals," *Seattle Times*, August 26, 2014, http://www.seattletimes.com/opinion/guest-from-warriors-to-guardians-mdash-returning-american-police-culture-to-democratic-ideals/.

Chapter 17: Punishment

1. Roy Walmsley, *World Prison Population List*, 10th ed. (London: International Centre for Prison Studies, 2014), 1, http://www.apcca.org/uploads/10th_Edition_2013.pdf; Alexia D. Cooper, Matthew R. Durose, and Howard N. Snyder, "Recidivism of Prisoners Released in 30 States in 2005: Patterns from 2005 to 2010," Bureau of Justice Statistics, accessed June 3, 2015, http://www.bjs.gov/index.cfm?ty=pbdetail&iid=4987; "PREA Data Collection Activities, 2014," Bureau of Justice Statistics, NCJ 245694, May 2014, http://www.bjs.gov/content/pub/pdf/pdca14.pdf; Heather C. West, "Prison Inmates at Midyear 2009—Statistical Tables," Bureau of Justice Statistics, NCJ 230113, June 2010, http://www.bjs.gov/content/pub/pdf/pim09st.pdf.

2. On forgiveness, punishment, and retribution, see Miroslav Volf, *Free of Charge: Giving and Forgiving in a Culture Stripped of Grace* (Grand Rapids: Zondervan, 2006), 127–91.

3. According to Criminal Justice Reports commissioned by the NAACP ("Death Row U.S.A.: Winter 2015," http://www.deathpenaltyinfo.org/documents/DRUSAWinter 2015.pdf), 35 percent of people executed since the 1976 reinstatement of the death penalty have been Black. Moreover, 42 percent of present death-row inmates are Black.

4. Federal mandatory minimum sentences for crack possession were abolished by the 2010 Fair Sentencing Act, which also reduced the disparity in sentencing treatment between crack and powder cocaine from 100:1 to 18:1 (see "The Fair Sentencing Act Corrects a Long-Time Wrong in Cocaine Cases," *Washington Post*, August 3, 2010, http://www.washingtonpost.com/wp-dyn/content/article/2010/08/02/AR2010080204 360.html). On the racial disparities of the "war on drugs" more generally, see Doris Maris Provine, "Race and Inequality in the War on Drugs," *Annual Review of Law and Social Science* 7 (2011): 41–60.

5. For example, between 1980 and 2010 Black youths were arrested for drug offenses at more than twice the rate of White youths, despite the fact that data suggest they are actually a little *less* likely to have used illegal drugs in any given month ("Report of the Sentencing Project to the United Nations Human Rights Committee Regarding Racial Disparities in the United States Criminal Justice System," The Sentencing Project, August 2013, 4, http://sentencingproject.org/doc/publications /rd_ICCPR%20Race%20and%20Justice%20Shadow%20Report.pdf). For more on racial profiling, see Andrew Gelman, Jeffrey Fagan, and Alex Kiss, "An Analysis of New York City Police Department's 'Stop-and-Frisk' Policy in the Context of Claims of Racial Bias," *Journal of the American Statistical Association* 102 (2007): 813–23. In January 2016 the *Guardian* reported that police officers killed 1,136 civilians in 2015. Of those, 223 were unarmed. And of those, 33.6 percent were Black. Approximately 12 percent of the US population is Black. See "The Counted," *Guardian*, http://www .theguardian.com/us-news/ng-interactive/2015/jun/01/the-counted-police-killings -us-database, for up-to-date information.

6. Research with jury-eligible participants in the United States shows a significant implicit association between Black faces and guilt and finds that this bias disposes would-be jurors to interpret ambiguous evidence as more indicative of guilt for Black than for White defendants (see Justin D. Levinson, Huajian Cai, and Danielle Young, "Guilty by Implicit Racial Bias: The Guilty/Not Guilty Implicit Association Test," *Ohio State Journal of Criminal Law* 8 [2010)]: 187–208).

7. The *Wall Street Journal* reported in 2013 that Black men are sentenced to 20 percent longer prison sentences than White men for similar crimes (Joe Palazzolo, "Racial Gap in Men's Sentencing," *Wall Street Journal*, February 14, 2013, http://www .wsj.com/articles/SB10001424127887324432004578304463789858002). For academic studies of disparate sentencing in general, see Brian D. Johnson, "Racial and Ethnic Disparities in Sentencing Departures across Modes of Conviction," *Criminology* 41 (2003): 449–89. Trial judges have been found to display implicit racial bias that can affect their judgments (see Jeffrey Rachlinski, Sheri Johnson, Andrew J. Wistrich, and Chris Guthrie, "Does Unconscious Racial Bias Affect Trial Judges?," *Notre Dame Law Review* 84 [2009]: 1195–246).

8. When criminologist Cheryl Lero Jonson analyzed numerous studies on imprisonment and reoffending, she found that the highest-quality studies showed that,

all else being equal, serving a prison sentence increased the likelihood of someone reoffending by 5 percent. Her findings are cited in Francis T. Cullen, Cheryl Lero Jonson, and Daniel S. Nagin, "Prisons Do Not Reduce Recidivism: The High Cost of Ignoring Science," *Prison Journal* 91, no. 3 (2011): 48S–65S. Prison might increase reoffending even more for drug offenders than for others (see Cassia Spohn and David Holleran, "The Effect of Imprisonment on Recidivism Rates of Felony Offenders: A Focus on Drug Offenders," *Criminology* 40 [2002]: 329–57).

9. For a portrait of what such a prison might look like, see the *New York Times Magazine* profile of Halden prison in Norway. Jessica Benko, "The Radical Humaneness of Norway's Halden Prison," *New York Times Magazine*, March 26, 2015, http://nyti.ms/1HMmyZ2.

10. See Michelle Alexander's devastating critique of the American penal system in *The New Jim Crow: Mass Incarceration in the Age of Colorblindness* (New York: New Press, 2012).

11. Suzy Khimm, "Will the Government Stop Using the Poor as a Piggy Bank?," MSNBC, September 9, 2014, http://www.msnbc.com/msnbc/will-the-government-stop-using-the-poor-piggy-bank.

Chapter 18: War

1. Milton Leitenberg, *Deaths in Wars and Conflicts in the 20th Century*, Cornell University Peace Studies Program Occasional Paper 29, 3rd ed., 1.

2. Ewen MacAskill and Ian Cobain, "British Forces' Century of Unbroken Warfare Set to End with Afghanistan Exit," *Guardian*, February 11, 2014, http://www.theguardian.com/uk-news/2014/feb/11/british-forces-century-warfare-end.

3. Stockholm International Peace Research Institute, SIPRI Military Expenditure Database, accessed June 1, 2015, http://www.sipri.org/research/armaments/milex/milex_database.

4. "God of peace" is one of the most common descriptions of God in the New Testament, especially the letters of Paul. In addition to the passages cited, it occurs in Rom. 16:20; 1 Cor. 14:33; 2 Cor. 13:11; Phil. 4:9; and 1 Thess. 5:23.

5. Oliver O'Donovan, *The Just War Revisited* (Cambridge: Cambridge University Press, 2003), 2. O'Donovan is loosely following some of John Milbank's ideas from *Theology and Social Theory* (Oxford: Blackwell, 1990).

6. The English term *pacifist* comes from the Latin word *pax*, meaning "peace."

7. Thomas Aquinas, *Summa Theologiae* II-II.40. The broader "treatise on charity" runs from question 23 to question 46.

8. Daniel M. Bell, "Just War as Christian Discipleship" (pamphlet 14 in the Renewing Radical Discipleship series, Ekklesia Pamphlets, ed. Daniel M. Bell Jr. and Joel Shuman [Eugene, OR: Wipf & Stock, 2005], http://www.ekklesiaproject.org/wp-content/uploads/2011/05/Ekklesia-14.pdf), offers a more extended but still accessible discussion of these criteria.

9. Augustine, *Letter* 189.6, in *Political Writings*, ed. E. M. Atkins and R. J. Dodaro (Cambridge: Cambridge University Press, 2001).

10. See Miroslav Volf, *Exclusion and Embrace: A Theological Exploration of Identity, Otherness, and Reconciliation* (Nashville: Abingdon, 1996), 275–306. While writing that book, my (Miroslav's) strong sense was that war could never be an instance of loving one's enemies, an indispensable condition for a war to be justifiable

on Christian grounds (a point on which Ryan and I agree); I am still hard-pressed to find one example of such war. Theoretically at least, such war is possible, so in the present text I am keeping that option open.

11. Bell, "Just War as Christian Discipleship," 5.

Chapter 19: Torture

1. This definition might not cover everything we would want to call torture, but it highlights the most salient feature of torture in the world today.

2. Accurate overall data on torture are nearly impossible to gather. See Amnesty International, *Report 2014/15: The State of the World's Human Rights* (London: Amnesty International, 2015), https://www.amnesty.org/en/documents/pol10/0001/2015 /en/, for information collected from nearly every country in the world.

3. It's quite possible that some forms of coercion in interrogation are not torture but are still wrong. This question would not be able to identify them.

4. See the selections of the *Theodosian Code* and Innocent's *Ad extirpanda* in Edward Peters, *Torture*, expanded ed. (Philadelphia: University of Pennsylvania Press, 1999), 212–14, 236–37.

5. Both a 2009 Pew survey and a 2014 Washington Post/ABC poll found that over 60 percent of White evangelicals believed that torture of suspected terrorists could be justified "often" or "sometimes" ("The Religious Dimensions of the Torture Debate," Pew Research Center, updated May 7, 2009, http://www.pewforum.org/2009/04/29/the -religious-dimensions-of-the-torture-debate/; "CIA Interrogations: The Ends Justify the Means," *Washington Post*, December 2014, http://apps.washingtonpost.com/g /page/politics/washington-post-abc-news-poll/1514/).

6. "Senate Report on CIA Torture Program," CNN, December 9, 2014, http://www .cnn.com/interactive/2014/12/politics/torture-report/; cf. Mark A. Costanzo and Ellen Gerrity, "The Effects and Effectiveness of Using Torture as an Interrogation Device: Using Research to Inform the Policy Debate," *Social Issues and Policy Review* 3 (2009): 182–85, https://www.cgu.edu/pdffiles/sbos/costanzo_effects_of_interrogation.pdf.

Chapter 20: Freedom of Religion (and Irreligion)

1. For the figures on government restrictions of religion and religiously moti-vated assault, see "Religious Hostilities Reach Six-Year High," Pew Research Center, January 14, 2014, http://www.pewforum.org/2014/01/14/religious-hostilities-reach-six -year-high/. On Indian anticonversion laws, see Shoaib Daniyal, "As Clamour to Ban Conversion Grows, a Reminder: Five Indian States Have Already Done So," *Scroll.in*, September 15, 2014, http://scroll.in/article/679080/as-clamour-to-ban-conversion -grows-a-reminder-five-indian-states-have-already-done-so. On French religious sym-bols laws, see "Resources on Faith, Ethics and Public Life: France," Berkley Center for Religion, Peace and World Affairs, accessed June 4, 2015, http://berkleycenter .georgetown.edu/resources/france. A new wave of controversy erupted in 2015 when a Muslim schoolgirl was sent home for wearing an ankle-length skirt (Alissa J. Rubin, "French School Deems Teenager's Skirt an Illegal Display of Religion," *New York Times*, April 29, 2015, http://nyti.ms/1zqrBPU). For the rates of harassment of Mus-lims and Christians, see "Rising Restrictions on Religion—One-Third of the World's